BEST OF TIMES:

The Story of

CHARLES
DICKENS

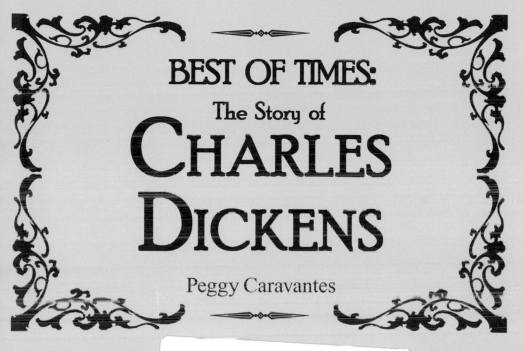

BEST OF TIMES:
The Story of
CHARLES
DICKENS

Peggy Caravantes

MORGAN REYNOLDS
PUBLISHING

Greensboro, North Carolina

WORLD WRITERS

CHARLES DICKENS

JANE AUSTEN

STEPHEN KING

RALPH ELLISON

ROBERT FROST

BEST OF TIMES: THE STORY OF CHARLES DICKENS

Copyright © 2005 by Peggy Caravantes

To my grandchildren—Katie, Michael, and Chris.
You light up my life!

Library of Congress Cataloging-in-Publication Data

Caravantes, Peggy, 1935-
    Best of times : the story of Charles Dickens / Peggy Caravantes.— 1st ed.
        p. cm.
Includes bibliographical references and index.
    ISBN-10: 1-931798-68-0 (lib. bdg.)
    ISBN-13: 978-1-931798-68-6 (lib. bdg.)
    1. Dickens, Charles, 1812-1870—Juvenile literature. 2. Novelists,
English—19th century—Biography—Juvenile literature. I. Title.
    PR4581.C37 2005
    823'.8—dc22

                        2005008405

Printed in the United States of America
First Edition

CONTENTS

One

Early Years

C ut the paper, cover the pot, tie the string, paste a label. Cut the paper, cover the pot, tie the string, paste a label. Paying little attention to the crowd watching him through the window of Warren's Blacking Factory, Charles Dickens forced himself to focus on the monotonous task of preparing pots of black shoe polish. If he slapped and pasted the labels on fast enough and loud enough, he could ignore the squeaking and scuffling sounds of the gray rats that swarmed in the cellar of the tumbledown old house that had been converted to a factory. And if he pushed himself to finish more pots today than yesterday, he could avoid thinking about his father, John Dickens, who had been taken to Marshalsea, London's debtors' prison. According to the

Opposite: *Charles Dickens.* (Courtesy of Victoria & Albert Museum, London / Art Resource.)

Warren's Blacking Factory in Hungerford Stairs, where Dickens worked as a child. (Greater London Record Office)

custom of the times, his mother and his younger brothers and sisters had moved into the prison with Mr. Dickens. But twelve-year-old Charles had been left to take care of himself.

Charles hated the factory but he dreaded even more going home to his lonely room. He was often hungry, since the few shillings he earned each day were not enough to buy a decent meal. Charles grew sadder and sadder but shared his agony with no one. In later years, he wrote: "That I suffered in secret, and that I suffered exquisitely, no one ever knew but I. How much I suffered, it is . . . utterly beyond my power to tell." This short period of his life, lasting less than a year, had a profound effect on the man and the writer that Charles Dickens became.

Charles John Huffam Dickens, who never used his

Charles's father, John Dickens.

two middle names, was born to John and Elizabeth Barrow Dickens on February 7, 1812, in Portsmouth, England. He arrived eighteen months after the birth of the Dickenses' first child, Frances Elizabeth (Fanny).

John Dickens was the second son of two highly placed servants in the home of a member of Parliament, Lord Crewe. With Crewe's backing, John received appointment as a clerk in the Navy Pay Office at the age of eighteen. He worked there for six years before he wed twenty-year-old Elizabeth. John had high aspirations for himself and his family. Unfortunately, he was also a poor manager of his own finances.

In September 1813, Charles's brother Alfred was born but died in infancy. Soon afterwards, John Dickens

The British port of Chatham, located approximately thirty miles southeast of London. (Library of Congress)

was transferred to London, where he earned less pay. In addition to his wife and two children, John Dickens supported Mary Allen, Elizabeth's widowed sister, whose husband had died at sea. Another daughter, Letitia Mary, was added to the crowded household on April 23, 1816. John Dickens was soon taking out small loans from tradespeople for goods and services—loans he had trouble repaying.

In March 1817, the Pay Office again transferred John Dickens, this time out of London to Chatham, a seaport near Rochester. This new job meant more money, and the family moved into a large house at 2 Ordnance Terrace,

The Dickens home on Ordnance Terrace in Chatham. Number 2 is the second house from the left.

across from an open field. Five-year-old Charles spent hours outdoors, absorbing the sights, sounds, and smells. He was a remarkably observant child with a keen memory. Charles was small for his age, not strong or athletic. However, he easily made friends with other children and entertained his playmates with stories and comic songs. In the early years in Chatham, his mother taught him the alphabet and the basics of reading.

John Dickens's spending habits—including the employment of two household servants—began to catch up with him. The family moved three times, and tradesmen trying to collect unpaid loans sent John Dickens into hiding. Tension hung over the family.

The first school that Charles and his older sister Fanny attended was on Rome Street. During the family's last two years in Chatham, Charles transferred to a school run by William Giles, a young Baptist minister who had attended Oxford University. Giles recognized and encouraged the boy's intelligence and imagination.

Charles loved to read and had free access to his father's collection of books and magazines. He and his father discussed the books as they walked about Chatham. John Dickens shared with his son his own ambitions, fueling the young boy's dreams of wealth, position, and property. They often strolled by a mansion, Gad's Hill Place, and John told Charles that if he worked hard enough, he could own a house like that someday.

In the nineteenth century, Britain had an entrenched class system with distinct upper, middle, and lower classes. Each had its own rank, living conditions, manners, and social life. What mobility there was between classes was mostly downward.

The upper class—aristocrats and gentry—owned large amounts of property and were England's governing class. The middle class was comprised of lawyers, doctors, teachers, merchants, military officers, and industrialists. At the beginning of the Victorian era, the middle class had no political power and no rank. However, by the end of the nineteenth century, this class had grown tremendously in influence and in size. The middle class began to copy the language and manners of the upper class and to pressure them to share political power.

The poor, which included tenant farmers, farm laborers, and uneducated factory workers, had little chance

for advancement. There was scant sympathy for their plight because of the nineteenth-century belief that poverty was the result of sin or indolence. Many lived in conditions unimaginable today.

Although John Dickens hovered between the poor and the lower middle classes, he held out to his son the dream of owning property, of becoming a part of the upper middle class. Even as a boy, Charles vowed to himself to realize that dream.

The Dickens family continued to grow. Harriet was born in 1819 and Frederick in 1821. John Dickens resorted to borrowing money from family and friends. In 1822, the Navy Pay Office transferred John Dickens back to London. The family's financial situation became more difficult as John again took a cut in pay.

In the early nineteenth century, the population of London was about 1.5 million. The Industrial Revolution had attracted thousands of people into the city where they lived in dense tenement housing. The city was extremely dirty—people threw garbage in the streets and dumped raw sewage directly into the river. The importance of hygiene was not yet understood, leading to regular epidemics of fatal diseases, including cholera and typhoid. No laws existed to regulate labor, so people, including children as young as three or four, worked sixteen- or seventeen-hour days, often in unsafe conditions. But for the rich or reasonably well off, London was a bustling city of excitement and fun. There was a booming theater district and plenty of fashionable shops.

The Dickenses settled in Camden Town on the city's outskirts, on a quiet street lined with cheaply built small cottages nestled beneath shade trees. Camden was a respectable enough area, separated from London by open fields, wasteland, and partially built-up areas. Charles spent hours walking, carefully observing all the people he encountered and taking special note of their facial expressions, speaking styles, mannerisms, and gestures. He did not attend school but amused himself by acting in plays he imagined or by writing out sketches of the neighborhood. He helped his mother by running errands and taking care of his younger brothers and sisters. Writing in later years, Dickens recalled: "What would I have given, if I had anything to give, to have been sent back to any other school, to have been taught something anywhere?"

The Royal Academy of Music accepted Charles's

older sister, Fanny, as a boarding pupil to study piano. The difference in the siblings' situations embittered the young Charles, who so wanted an education for himself.

When circumstances did not improve for the Dickens family, Charles's mother, Elizabeth, took matters into her own hands. She proposed that the Dickenses acquire a much larger house and convert it into

Charles's mother, Elizabeth Dickens.

a boarding school. The family moved to 4 Gower Street North, where Mrs. Dickens placed a brass plate near the front door announcing MRS. DICKENS'S ESTABLISHMENT. She sent Charles to distribute fliers announcing the opening of her school, but no one ever attended.

The family began to sell their household goods, often using Charles to negotiate the transactions. He became well acquainted with the indignity of pawnshop transactions and with his father's temper. The already-quiet boy became more withdrawn as the family's financial situation tightened.

A family member by marriage, James Lamert, offered to get Charles a job at Warren's Blacking Factory, where Lamert worked. Not until 1833 would Britain pass the first of its factory acts, designed to restrict the working hours of young children. However, Charles was still surprised that his parents raised no objections to their twelve-year-old son going to work in a factory: "My father and mother were quite satisfied. They could hardly have been more so, if I had been twenty years of age, distinguished at a grammar-school and going to Cambridge."

Mr. Lamert allowed Charles to eat upstairs with him instead of with the other boys and planned to use lunchtime to educate him. The boys resented Charles's privileged status and mockingly referred to him as the "young gentleman." When Lamert became too busy to tutor Charles, he moved him to the same floor as the other boys.

Charles's biggest fear was that he would lose his lower-middle-class station. The stress of the job, the worry about his position in life, and the ill will of the other boys finally made him sick. One day, Charles fell to the floor with a sharp pain in his side. An older boy, Bob Fagin, went to his aid and continued to watch out for Charles. The pain in Charles's side would recur throughout his lifetime whenever he became anxious. It was probably the result of kidney stones, but Dickens saw it as a more symbolic injury.

Because of complaints filed by his creditors, John

Dickens was sentenced to debtors' prison. This was a fairly common practice of the times, and Dickens knew he could file for relief under the Insolvent Debtors Act. However, he worried that news of his arrest would get him fired from the Navy Pay Office. Accordingly, he obtained a letter from a doctor certifying he had a chronic urinary infection that would keep him from working and applied for a pension. Because the courts worked slowly, the Navy Pay Office had not yet learned about his situation.

In accordance with the custom of the times, the family moved into John Dickens's prison cell, except Charles,

Frank Hall's nineteenth-century oil painting shows a scene from Newgate Prison, a dismal, unsanitary place that served as a debtors' prison, a holding pen for those awaiting execution, and a place of detention for suspects who had not yet been tried. (Royal Holloway College, Egham)

who stayed with an old woman who boarded three other children. He spent long days at the factory and nights in his lonely room. He quickly learned to be self-reliant and to find solace in routines. He carefully divided up his pay to ensure it would last the week. He ate alone in restaurants and spent long hours walking the dirty city streets, absorbing all that he saw.

On Sundays, Charles and Fanny—who was still at the Royal Academy of Music—visited their parents. There, Charles enjoyed a heartier meal than the scant ones his few shillings a day provided. Other than those once-weekly visits, he recalled that he had "no advice, no counsel, no encouragement, no consolation, no support, from anyone that I can call to mind, so help me God." His father finally recognized his son's sense of abandonment and managed to secure him lodging on the south side of the river closer to the prison.

While waiting to hear the results of his pension application, John Dickens continued to work to gain release from prison through the Insolvent Debtors Act. He finally reached an agreement with his creditors. On May 28, 1824, John Dickens was released from Marshalsea. Ten months later, he began to receive a pension from the Navy Pay Office.

Even after his family was out of jail, Charles continued to work at Warren's. Once the elder Dickens's pension came through, however, John Dickens wrote an irate letter to James Lamert complaining that Charles had to work under poor conditions and on display. Lamert responded with an angry note of his own, saying that Charles was fired.

Since Charles's mother enjoyed the extra money her son contributed to the household expenses, she wanted him to continue to work. She contacted Lamert, the son of her sister Mary's husband, and soothed his hurt feelings. She got him to agree to let Charles return to work. Charles later declared: "I never afterwards forgot, I never shall forget, I never can forget, that my mother was warm for my being sent back."

But John Dickens refused to allow Charles to return to Warren's. Instead he enrolled him at the nearby Wellington House Academy. Although returning to school excited Charles, he felt some uneasiness. He realized that the past year had provided him experiences different from those of the other boys. In the largely autobiographical novel *David Copperfield,* Dickens created a character that endured a similar experience:

> I got a little the better of my uneasiness when I went to school next day, and a good deal the better next day, and so shook it off by degrees that in less than a fortnight I was quite at home and happy, among my new companions. I was awkward enough in their games, and backward enough in their studies; but custom would improve me in the first respect, I hoped, and hard work in the second. Accordingly, I went to work very hard, both in play and in earnest . . . and in a very little while the [past] became so strange to me that I hardly believed in it, while my present life grew

so familiar that I seemed to have been leading it a long time.

At Wellington, Charles Dickens hoped to regain the respectability that he felt he had lost at Warren's. It was important to him to fit in, to look and act just like the other boys—none of whom had ever labored in a factory. He entered fully into the school's activities, training white mice that the boys hid in their desks and drawers, staging plays in toy theaters, or writing stories for the

Wellington House Academy on Hampstead Road in London. Charles attended the school for approximately two years.

This unsigned miniature is thought to be the first portrait done of Charles Dickens. (Dickens House Museum, London)

school paper. Wellington Academy was not a top-notch school. The headmaster, Mr. Jones, took a cruel pleasure in punishing the boys. He hit their palms with a wooden ruler and was noted for "viciously drawing a pair of pantaloons tight with one of his large hands, and caning the wearer with the other."

After Charles started at Wellington, he and his parents never mentioned his months at Warren's. However, Charles had learned a hard lesson: happiness can disappear without warning. By resuming his education, Charles Dickens believed that he could still fulfill his ambition to become an educated gentleman. He wanted enough education to hold a good job, so that he would never experience the shame of debtors' prison or working in a factory again. Charles stayed at the academy until he was almost fifteen years old.

It was another downturn in his father's finances that forced Charles to withdraw from the school, effectively ending his formal education. Always in need of more money, the forty-one-year-old John Dickens learned the complicated Gurney's shorthand system and became a reporter for *The British Press*. The newspaper folded after only a few months. Adding to his mounting debts was the birth of Augustus Dickens in March 1827, the Dickenses' seventh child in seventeen years. As Augustus began to talk, he mangled his nickname "Moses" to "Boses," later shortened to "Boz"—a name that would in a few years make his brother Charles famous.

Two

Back to Work

━━━◆◆◆━━━

I n May 1827, at age fifteen, Charles went to work
as a junior clerk for the legal firm of Ellis &
Blackmore. His mother had met Edward Blackmore,
a junior partner, at her aunt's house, where Blackmore
boarded. Mrs. Dickens urged Blackmore to hire Charles.
Blackmore, who thought Charles was "exceedingly good
looking and clever," agreed. Charles's job was to regis-
ter wills, serve papers, and carry documents from the law
offices to the courts. He was by now close to his adult
height of five feet nine, and was already paying close
attention to his dress. He affected a uniform with a
military look, as was the fashion of the day, and stood
as straight as his shoulders would allow.

To offset the dullness of his daytime tasks, Charles
walked around London in the evenings and attended a

theater performance almost every night. He had been an avid actor since childhood and probably took part in local amateur productions.

Dickens's father's debts and his family's constant struggle to get by had imbued in Charles a driving work ethic. He decided to follow his father's lead and began to study the complex Gurney shorthand in order to become a reporter. Two months before his seventeenth birthday, Charles mastered all of the system's lines and squiggles and left Ellis & Blackmore. For a short time he worked for another lawyer, Charles Molloy. When a

A page of Charles's shorthand notes. (Dickens House Museum, London)

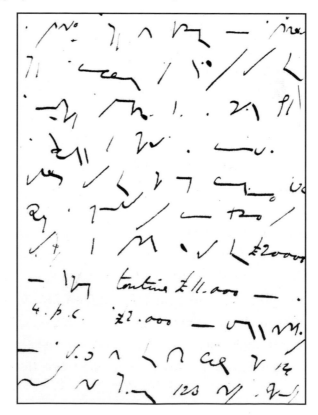

Charles Dickens at age eighteen, as painted by Janet Barrow. (Dickens House Museum, London)

family friend offered to let Charles share his rented space at a group of courts, Charles left Molloy and began freelance reporting legal proceedings. He quickly became noted for the speed with which he took notes and for the accuracy of his reports.

On his eighteenth birthday, Charles Dickens applied for a reading card at the British Museum Library, where he spent many hours completing his education. His job took him all over the city. He paid close attention to everything he saw and heard, and soon his head was

The House of Commons at Westminster, where Dickens worked as a reporter.
(Mansell Collection)

filled with observations and experiences. At age nineteen, while still reporting, Dickens began to work for the *Mirror of Parliament,* the newspaper where his father now worked.

The younger Dickens recorded speeches in the House of Commons, and the newspaper printed these parliamentary reports verbatim. The work was difficult and often dull. Reporters were crowded into a poorly lit corridor at the back of the house, often balancing their notebooks on their knees. The speeches they recorded were sometimes hard to hear. Still, it was an excellent education in politics.

England was rapidly changing in the 1800s. The Industrial Revolution led to huge population increases in urban areas like London. More people meant more problems, and the 1830s saw a Parliament elected that was committed to reform. Voting rights were restored to Catholics, and the slave trade was soon officially abolished. Attention was beginning to be paid to the plight of the urban poor, though reform would be slow in coming.

Dickens earned a decent salary as a reporter, enough to support himself and still enjoy the entertainment of the day. He soon fell in with a crowd of young men of similar tastes. They enjoyed drinking and eating and merrymaking, as well as attending the theater. Dickens was still enamored of the stage and thrilled to be invited to audition for a part in Sheridan Knowles's *The Hunchback* at Covent Garden Theatre. On the day of the tryouts,

London's famous Covent Garden Theatre was destroyed by fire in 1808 but was quickly rebuilt. This painting shows the theater as it would have looked in the late 1820s.

he was forced to cancel because of a bad cold and never again attempted to make the leap from amateur theatrical productions to professional. In later years, an old stagehand lamented to Dickens, "Ah, Mr. Dickens, it was a sad loss to the public when you took to writing."

But writing was proving to be Dickens's real talent. In March 1832, he took on additional reporting duties for an evening paper, *True Sun*. This paper did not prove successful, and so, at age twenty-three Charles became a full-time employee at the daily *Morning Chronicle*. It was around this time that he first began to write in earnest. His head was full of all the people and places he had seen, and he had a keen sense of drama— especially melodrama. In his room at night or in between assignments at the paper, he began writing down the stories that filled his head.

When Dickens was just eighteen, he had met and fallen in love with a woman two years his senior, Maria Beadnell. In a short time he became consumed with his passion for her—an obsession that lasted four years. Dickens idealized Beadnell as the perfect woman, someone who would provide the mothering he so missed from his childhood. Unfortunately, Beadnell was not in the least nurturing. A charming, petite, brunette, blue-eyed beauty, she wanted only to have a good time and to be admired by numerous adoring suitors. The Beadnell family, with three daughters of marriageable age, entertained a variety of young men in their home. Mrs. Beadnell, a class-conscious woman, welcomed Dickens,

Maria Beadnell in 1835.

a bachelor with good manners and entertaining stories, into the circle as another guest, but she did not envision him as a prospective son-in-law.

Mr. Beadnell was a clerk in a bank managed by a family member. The Beadnells thus represented a class to which Dickens, a young journalist, aspired but did not belong. Although she flirted with him, Maria never took Dickens seriously. Finally, his declarations of love and the gifts that he brought their youngest daughter began to concern the Beadnells. About the same time, Charles's father was once again declared an insolvent debtor. Seeing this fact published in the *London Gazette* provided the impetus for the Beadnells to separate Maria from her most persistent suitor. They sent her to Paris,

France, to attend finishing school. Twenty-three years later, when Charles Dickens wrote the word "Paris," he recalled, "My existence was once entirely uprooted and my whole Being blighted by the Angel of my soul being sent there to finish her education."

Beadnell returned to London in early 1833 but was cold and indifferent toward Dickens. For some reason, though, perhaps just for the intrigue involved, she agreed to exchange secret letters with him. A mutual friend and one of the Beadnells' maids carried the letters between them. Encouraged by her agreement to the secret plot, Dickens waited expectantly for Beadnell to acknowledge his love. She attended a coming-of-age party for his twenty-first birthday and then, in a letter a few days later, referred to him as a "boy." Dickens was hurt and upset. His agonized response made her angry.

Beadnell came from a secure middle-class environment. Dickens never understood that she was unlikely to marry a young man who was her inferior both economically and socially. In his last letter to her, Dickens exclaimed, "I never have loved and I never can love any human creature breathing but yourself." Heartbroken, he threw himself into his writing.

In 1833, Charles Dickens saw his first piece of fiction in print. In November, he dropped a story, "Dinner at Poplar Walk," into the mailbox at *Monthly Magazine*. A month later, he visited a bookstore where he discovered the December issue included his story.

"Dinner at Poplar Walk" was a light piece similar in

Dickens placing his first literary contribution in the editor's box.

This cartoon depicting Dickens submitting his first literary sketches was created in 1835. (Courtesy of Getty Images.)

style to the theatrical productions Dickens so enjoyed. It showcased the humor that would become the author's hallmark, though there was little else about it to indicate Dickens would go on to become a literary star. In the coming months, he would write eight more stories for *Monthly Magazine,* though he would not be paid for any of them.

Soon after his first story was published, Dickens discovered that his father was once again deeply in debt. This time, Dickens feared he might be held liable for some of his father's expenditures. John Dickens spent a frantic weekend trying to scrape together enough money to stave off his creditors, including the landlord. When no word came from his father, Dickens was sent out and found John in a sponging house, a holding place for debtors to give them a chance to settle their debts before they are taken to prison.

Dickens managed to put together enough cash to get his father released but did not have sufficient funds to pay the overdue rent. Charles had to find a place where his mother and brothers and sisters could stay—John Dickens had disappeared somewhere his creditors could not find him. This was only the first of many times that Dickens had to rescue his father from financial disaster.

Dickens was an extremely hard worker and seemed incapable of refusing an opportunity that might advance his career or earn him more money. The editors of the *Morning Chronicle* decided to start a later edition, the *Evening Chronicle,* and appointed George Hogarth editor. Hogarth recognized Dickens's writing ability and encouraged him to write about London life for the paper. Inspired by memories of his walks around London and his remarkable capacity to remember names, faces, and personalities, Dickens wrote numerous sketches of city life. On each one he signed the pen name "Boz" in honor of his youngest brother.

Readers loved the sketches of ordinary people and the events in their lives. They were captivated by Dickens's eye for spot-on detail and his humorous prose. Everyone wondered who "Boz" was. The popularity of his pieces brought about a salary increase, and by age twenty-three Charles made more money than the best salary his father had ever received from the Navy Pay Office.

George Hogarth had a large family and frequently invited guests to his home. Dickens became a regular visitor, accepted into the happy family that included sisters Catherine, Mary, Georgina, and a toddler, Helen. Catherine was a pretty girl with a small mouth, slightly upturned nose, and sleepy eyes. With her quiet ways and eagerness to please, she fulfilled Dickens's need for someone to cater to him. She seemed to like him more as they became better acquainted.

The two were nothing alike. Dickens had to be moving constantly; Catherine was slow. He was still as slim as a boy; she was plump. He knew exactly what he wanted to achieve; she was unsure about herself. He believed that he could accomplish anything; she was not ambitious. Catherine in no way resembled Beadnell. She would not remind Dickens of that lost love but could provide him a home and family. In May 1835, just one year after giving up the pursuit of Maria Beadnell, Charles Dickens became engaged to Catherine Hogarth.

Catherine's new fiancé was devoted to his work and often skipped the traditional nightly courtship visit. She

Young Catherine Hogarth in 1835, shortly before her marriage to Dickens.

was somewhat disappointed by how little attention he paid her, but generally the young couple got along well. Dickens was very sensitive to any insult—real or perceived—and one of their first fights concerned whether or not she was allowed to criticize him. The next day, Catherine received a letter containing a severe scolding and setting out the rules for their relationship. In it, Dickens stated that such an incident must not occur again because she would get no second chances.

Catherine feared responding with her true feelings and instead pacified her angry beau.

Dickens worked extremely long hours, often rising early to write before going to work, then returning home to put in more time at his desk. He missed Catherine and wrote to her: "I should like to have you by me—*so* much . . . God bless you dearest Pig. How long it is, since I saw you! Never mind—it will soon be over."

In October 1835, publisher John Macrone approached Dickens about collecting the articles he had written into a two-volume work called *Bubbles from the Bwain of Boz*. Dickens was thrilled by the idea, though he did not like the title and suggested *Sketches by Boz* instead. The sketches represented Dickens's extensive study of the people of the lower middle class and of the poor. When he wrote about social conditions, he drew from a wealth of examples collected since childhood. The descriptions, with their carefully selected details, were his first social commentaries. They were also funny, offering readers a chance to laugh as they peered into the lives of those around them.

Dickens took the time to revise the sketches before publication, making sure to erase any passages that indicated they had originally been published in the paper. This attention to detail was typical of him and marked his professionalism both as a reporter and as a writer. The book was published on February 7, 1836, Dickens's twenty-fourth birthday, and contained illus-

The title page of Dickens's first collection, Sketches by Boz.

trations by George Cruikshank. The publisher purchased the copyright for one hundred pounds.

In the same month that *Sketches* appeared, Dickens moved to better living quarters at Furnival's Inn. There he was approached by the publishers Thomas Chapman and William Hall, who asked Dickens to write a monthly serial to accompany Robert Seymour's illustrations about the comic adventures of some members of a sporting club, a popular subject in the 1830s. Dickens jumped at the opportunity but convinced the publishers the illustrations should be secondary to the text.

Furnival's Inn, Holborn, where Dickens lived from 1834 to 1837.

The publishers agreed to pay Dickens fourteen pounds for each installment. The first four hundred copies of *The Posthumous Papers of the Pickwick Club* were issued on March 31, 1836. Samuel Pickwick and his friends had hilarious adventures and run-ins with all manner of characters, all drawn from Dickens's fertile imagination. Readers loved the way Dickens poked fun at the sporting club members' blundering attempts to copy the upper class.

This publication was the first of Dickens's books to take advantage of the publishing revolution occurring in the Victorian era. Increased literacy rates, along with new print and illustration technologies, had given rise to an increased demand for literature that both informed and entertained. The growing middle class formed the largest audience.

However, owning books was still a luxury. Publishing was expensive, so many readers rented novels from circulating libraries. Such rentals produced a more stable income for the publishers than did individual sales. Publishers encouraged authors to produce long novels written in three separate volumes, thus tripling the fees as readers rented one volume at a time. Serialization offered a more economical alternative to readers. When serialized novels appeared in a magazine, readers could purchase the installments and get the rest of the magazine's contents as well.

Serialization gave Dickens more freedom with the story line of *The Pickwick Papers*. He was able to alter the direction of the story line in response to public opinion. Each episode was about 12,000 words long. Dickens was writing extremely quickly, yet still managing to be funny, topical, and vividly descriptive. He also began to try to exercise more control over the illustrations that accompanied his text. After one such confrontation with Seymour, during which Dickens, backed by Chapman and Hall, suggested a change to a picture, Seymour went home to his garden and committed suicide. That he had a history of mental instability did not make his actions much easier to bear.

Under ordinary circumstances Seymour's death might have ended publication of the *Pickwick* installments. But the publishers had great faith in Dickens and began interviewing other illustrators. They hired Hablot Knight Browne, who took on the pseudonym "Phiz" to go along with Dickens's "Boz." Browne was a quiet, obliging man and made an excellent counterpart to the mercurial, often temperamental Dickens. The plump, bald figure of Samuel Pickwick, businessman and confirmed bachelor, delighted readers, and the name attached itself to all kinds of goods: Pickwick cigars, Pickwick hats, Pickwick canes with tassels, and Pickwick coats cut in a certain style.

By the sixth installment, it was clear success was assured—particularly due to a new character, Sam Weller, a comic servant who was as worldly as his master Pickwick was naïve. Dickens shifted the emphasis of the stories from the sporting club's adventures to the relationship between Pickwick and Weller. Weller became a symbol of the British poor and reflects their dark sense of humor with his "Wellerisms." As Pickwick and his companions travel from place to place, Weller becomes Dickens's voice, satirically commenting on the social pretensions of the people he encounters and on the social abuses of the day. Time and time again, the streetwise Weller rescues Pickwick from the British court system. These encounters allowed Dickens to express his disdain for the English legal system by parodying its procedures and skewering its stereotypes.

People of all ages and classes loved the book. Dickens found a particular following among the poor, perhaps because he captured so accurately what a farce it could be to be alive at the time. An observer described how

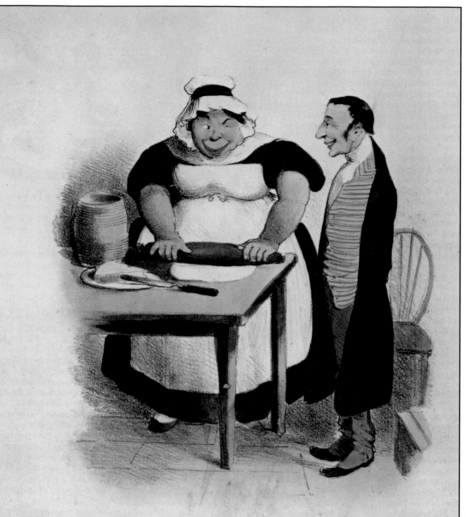

I say, Sally, wot a good thing it would be if ve vos to jine your £100 wot the Old Man left yer and the £30 youve got in the Savings Bank & the £10 a year wot Missis left yer and them ere 5 Sovereigns wot young Master guv yer, to my *seven shillings & Sixpence* a veek & the Christmas Box wot Master's a going to give me ___ ve might then open a Beer shop!

London W Spooner 377 Strand.

Cockney humor — the use of dialect and characters from Britain's serving class — became the basis for much of Dickens's early work, such as this sketch from Pickwick. (Victoria & Albert Museum, London) "needy admirers flattened their noses against the book-sellers' windows eager to secure a good look at the etchings and to peruse every line of the letterpress that might be exposed to view, frequently reading it aloud to applauding bystanders . . . so great was the craze, *Pickwick Papers* secured far more attention than was given to the ordinary politics of the day."

The final installment, in November 1837, sold 40,000 copies—one hundred times the initial printing. Chapman and Hall gave a dinner to celebrate the success and to honor Dickens. William Giles, Charles's old schoolmaster, sent Dickens a small snuffbox engraved to "The Inimitable Boz." Dickens prized that name for himself above all others.

Within a few days of the publication of the first installment of *The Pickwick Papers*, Charles Dickens married Catherine Hogarth at St. Luke's Church, Chelsea, on April 2, 1836. They honeymooned in a village near the place where Dickens had spent his early, happy childhood years. When the newlyweds returned home, they lived in Dickens's quarters at Furnival's Inn, where they had three rooms on the third floor and a basement kitchen. Mary, Catherine's sixteen-year-old sister, came to stay with them, a means of relieving overcrowding in the Hogarth household.

Dickens seemed unable to turn down any offers. Although he had never followed up on his ambition for a career as an actor, he became a playwright, writing a comedy, *The Strange Gentleman;* an operetta, *The Vil-*

lage Coquettes; and a farce, *Is She His Wife?* None of these was a tremendous success, and it was clear that Dickens's real strength was in the novel.

In May 1836, Dickens agreed to publisher John Macrone's proposal to write a three-volume novel, *Gabriel Vardon, the Locksmith of London,* later retitled *Barnaby Rudge: A Tale of the Riots of Eighty.* The contract, which would pay Dickens two hundred pounds for the first one thousand copies and half the profits after that, called for a November completion. Dickens liked the idea of being able to share in the profits and made this agreement without consulting anyone, including his other publishers, Chapman and Hall.

In August, publisher Richard Bentley presented Dickens the opportunity to become the first editor of *Bentley's Miscellany,* an illustrated monthly magazine. That fall, based upon *Pickwick's* popularity, Chapman and Hall proposed that Dickens do a sequel to *Pickwick.* Dickens accepted both offers and promptly became entangled in a web of contracts and agreements, all scheduled for completion on similar timelines—an impossible situation.

Dickens angered the owner of the *Evening Chronicle* by resigning without notice in order to try to meet these contractual obligations. Macrone got wind of his writer's multiple commitments and became anxious about Dickens's ability to produce *Barnaby Rudge.* Things were tense as Dickens was pressed from all sides about how he was going to satisfy all the people to whom he had promised work.

It was during this hectic time that Dickens met John Forster, a drama critic for the *Examiner*. Forster and Dickens had a lot in common. They were the same age, from similar backgrounds, and both interested in theater and literature. Forster soon came to be Dickens's primary advisor on all his professional activities and acted as Dickens's agent. Forster also edited many of Dickens's works, and their productive, though often dramatic, relationship would span the rest of their lives. Dickens entered into a comfortable routine. He rose early to write until mid-afternoon, then went riding with his friends, took dinner at a club, and usually attended the theater in the evening. Forster was one of the several young men

Dickens's friend John Forster. (Victoria & Albert Museum, London)

who made up his fun-loving circle.

Although Macrone was in the right, Forster somehow convinced him to allow Dickens to cancel the novel contract. By the time the negotiations were concluded, Macrone and Dickens were not speaking to each other. Dickens would soon earn a reputation as a difficult and obstinate writer. He was constantly afraid he was being taken advantage of or that he was not being paid the money he deserved. Dickens often relied on his gut instead of his head, and publishers were glad to have Forster serve as a more levelheaded intermediary.

In order to fulfill the terms of his agreement with Bentley, Dickens needed to write quickly. Even as he began his next novel, he was still writing installments of *The Pickwick Papers,* as well as editing the magazine. This work involved reading submitted manuscripts for possible publication, choosing the content for and editing each issue, and coordinating with the publishers. Now, Dickens added *Oliver Twist* to his plate as well.

Oliver Twist was one of the two novels promised to Bentley and the first to carry Dickens's real name instead of the pseudonym "Boz." The book appeared in twenty-four installments in *Bentley's Miscellany,* the first of which ran in February 1837. *Oliver Twist* took on two subjects Dickens considered evil: the 1834 Poor Law and the way the lives of London thieves were often glamorized in the popular literature of the day.

The Poor Law was ostensibly designed to combat the widespread poverty in England by establishing workhouses. Anyone in need could turn to a workhouse where, in exchange for their labor, they would be given the food or clothing they required. However, the Poor Law presented many problems: in order to encourage workhouse residents to find jobs of their own, workhouses were made to be extremely unpleasant environments. Families were separated when they entered—children taken from parents, then separated from each other. Further, no aid was allowed to a poor person who did not live in a workhouse.

Dickens used biting satire to criticize the persons who devised such a law. He also blamed the bureaucracy that administered the policies, not only in workhouses like the one described in *Oliver Twist* but in all types of institutions that crushed the human spirit. Dickens advocated for justice and mercy for these unfortunate victims of society.

Oliver Twist was the first of Dickens's innocent child protagonists who had to make their own way through a wicked world. When Oliver, a workhouse orphan, asks for more gruel—the thin, watery soup fed to the workers three times a day—Dickens vividly describes the scene in which Oliver's simple request is treated like a major uprising:

> [Oliver] rose from the table, and advancing to the master, basin and spoon in hand, said, somewhat alarmed at his own temerity: "Please, sir, I want some more." The master was a fat, healthy man, but he

turned very pale . . . The assistants were paralysed with wonder, the boys with fear.

"What!" said the master at length, in a faint voice.

"Please, sir," replied Oliver, "I want some more."

The master aimed a blow at Oliver's head with a ladle, pinioned him in his arms, and shrieked aloud for the beadle . . .

"I beg your pardon, sir! Oliver Twist has asked for more!"

This illustration from Oliver Twist *was done by George Cruikshank.* (Courtesy of Art Resource.)

There was a general start. Horror was depicted on every countenance.

"For more! . . . Do I understand that he asked for more after he had eaten the supper allotted by the dietary?"

"He did, sir . . ."

"That boy will be hung . . . I know that boy will be hung."

In contrast to the popular fiction of the day that often glorified thieves, Dickens showed their evil ways. Bill Sikes, who has lost all human feeling, represents the opposite end of the spectrum from Oliver's innocence. A brutal thief and murderer, he tries to carry out a scheme to corrupt Oliver by involving him in a robbery. Dickens wrote: "I wished to show, in little Oliver, the principle of good surviving through every adverse circumstance, and triumphing at last." Through the young Oliver's adversities, Dickens offered a new view to his readers of the life of the poor, as seen through the eyes of a child. Dickens so identified with his fictional character that, while writing, he again suffered the severe pains in his side first experienced in his childhood.

Oliver Twist, with its serious themes, was very different from the humorous escapades found in *The Pickwick Papers*. At first, public reception was cool. Lord Melbourne, Prime Minister of England from 1834 to 1841, commented: "I don't *like* those things. I wish to avoid them: I don't like them *in reality* and therefore I don't wish them represented." Yet Dickens developed the book's characters in such a compelling way that both the upper and middle classes were drawn into the story. This appeal to all types of people marked Dickens's early success as a writer. The same characteristics still draw modern readers to the story. *Oliver Twist* has been the subject of hundreds of stage adaptations, and more than twenty film versions have been produced. In Dickens's own time, the book helped to cement his reputation as one of the most popular writers of the day. More fame was to follow.

Three

Making a Name

O n January 6, 1837, Catherine delivered the
first of the couple's ten children. They chris
tened the boy Charles "Charley" Culliford
Boz Dickens. Dickens's sixteen-year-old brother Fred
came to live with them, and the family moved to a larger
house at 48 Doughty Street. Charles Dickens was an up-
and-coming young author with a family and ever-in-
creasing responsibilities. This transition was complicated by Catherine's ill health after Charley's birth and
Dickens's mercurial personality. Although he often was
the life of the party, a buoyant and boisterous merrymaker,
he was also prone to periods of withdrawal, which might
be called depression today.

In early May, the Dickens family suffered a terrible
blow when Catherine's sister, Mary, died at the age of

seventeen. She, along with Charles and Catherine, had just returned from St. James's Theatre, where they had seen a performance of Dickens's farce, *Is She His Wife?* As Charles and Catherine were getting ready for bed, they heard a choking cry. Dickens rushed to Mary's second-floor bedroom, where he found her collapsed on the floor. Doctors could do nothing for her. She had suffered a heart attack and died that afternoon in Dickens's arms. He removed from her finger a ring that he placed on his own hand, where he wore it the rest of his life.

Dickens bought a burial plot for Mary in Kensal Green Cemetery, where he planned to be buried next to her someday. He wrote to a friend: "The dear girl had been the grace and life of our home. . . . We might have known that we were too happy together to be long

Catherine Dickens's sister, Mary Hogarth.

Collins's Farm in Hampstead, where Mrs. Dickens went to live for a short while after the death of her sister Mary. (Museum of London)

without a change. . . . I have lost the dearest friend I ever had. Words cannot describe the pride I felt in her, and the devoted attachment I bore her."

Dickens's attachment to his wife's sister has long been a source of controversy. Some argue his feelings for her were largely paternal, while others see a romantic—if unconsummated—relationship. It's also possible that she represented the youth and innocence he so admired but never possessed. Dickens would often reincarnate Mary Hogarth in future books, keeping her memory alive in fiction.

Mary's death was difficult for Catherine. Dickens moved her, now pregnant with their second child, to a small farm in Hampstead to recover there. Catherine suffered a miscarriage, and Dickens missed, for the first

The young new queen of Great Britain, Victoria, on the day of her coronation in 1838.

time, the monthly installments of his two novels. Not until he was nearing his own death did Dickens again miss an installment.

In June 1837, King William IV died and was succeeded by his eighteen-year-old niece, Queen Victoria. Her coronation was cause for great rejoicing around the country as her subjects hoped she would usher in a new era of prosperity.

The Reform Bill of 1832 had greatly increased the number of citizens eligible to vote. However, a number of inequalities still remained, and a growing movement was agitating to have them addressed. Perhaps even more significant than their demands was the fact people were making them at all. The landed aristocracy's long control over British society was coming to an end. There was an increasing sense that the individual, no matter what his social or economic status, had value and political rights.

In the summer of 1837, Dickens began a tradition of taking his family to the sea for a restful vacation away from the city. Ensconced in a comfortable home in the quiet town of Broadstairs, Dickens could devote himself to his writing while his family enjoyed the fresh air. Many of their city friends came to visit, filling the Dickens household with the noise and excitement Charles thrived on. He often seemed more content in the company of his friends than of his family.

As Dickens continued to produce installments of *Oliver Twist,* he also began work on a new novel, *The Life and Adventures of Nicholas Nickleby.* The public's sympathetic reaction to the workhouse orphan Oliver Twist encouraged Dickens to focus this next novel on social issues. He had some concern about flooding the market with his work, and delayed beginning the novel by working on miscellaneous projects, including editing manuscripts for *Bentley's.*

The social issue Dickens dealt with in *Nicholas Nickleby* was the Yorkshire Schools, notorious for their abuse of the boys placed in their care. Dickens had known a youth that had attended one of the Yorkshire Schools. The boy told Dickens that he had suffered through a surgery to clean out an abscess that was performed with a small pocketknife. Dickens had never forgotten this story. A little research into the matter revealed that these so-called schools were often little more than prisons.

In this era before the concept of free, public education had been embraced, anywhere from two-thirds to three-fourths of working-class children did not attend school regularly. The most popular schools were "Sunday" schools, held on the one day a week children did not have to work. The instruction consisted of rudimentary reading skills, usually dedicated to deciphering the Bible.

Taking along his illustrator, Hablot Browne, Dickens assumed a fake name and set out to investigate the Yorkshire Schools. He managed to interview several people, including teachers and students, and was moved almost to tears at the sight of a graveyard for the boys who had died while enrolled. His subterfuge was eventually discovered, but Dickens got what he wanted: firsthand experience with the kind of people he intended to expose. His eye for detail and his remarkable memory would provide him with plenty of fodder.

In the end, *Nicholas Nickleby* was more than just an exposé of bad schools. In fact, the Yorkshire narrative took up only a few chapters. In an advertisement for the book, Dickens wrote: "It will be our aim to amuse, by producing a rapid succession of characters and incidents, and describing them as cheerfully and pleasantly as in us lies." He knew the way to keep readers would be by balancing his depiction of the social abuses with the comedy they had come to expect from the author of *Pickwick*.

This portrait was done to commemorate the completion of Nicholas Nickleby. *Despite Dickens's success, he remained sympathetic to the plight of the working class.* (Dickens House Museum, London)

Despite his tendency toward depression, Dickens was often a cheerful man. He loved to laugh and particularly enjoyed humor that was incongruous. He was an excellent mimic and kept his friends in stitches with his impersonations. *Nicholas Nickleby* provided Dickens fans with the kind of comic episodes they had come to expect.

The first of twenty sections of *Nicholas Nickleby* appeared in April 1838, just a month after Catherine Dickens gave birth to another baby girl—Mary (Mamie), named for her late aunt. *Nicholas Nickleby* was an instant hit. Dickens was by now an immensely popular figure in England. People called each other—and themselves—by his characters' names and affected his language and his characters' dress. Those who could not read could always find someone willing to read the installments to them, and those who could not afford the few cents it took to purchase the magazine pooled their money with friends. Dickens's widespread appeal made him the most well-known and best-loved writer of his generation. Soon after *Nicholas Nickleby* was published, most of the Yorkshire Schools were closed.

A few weeks before Christmas 1839, the Dickens family settled into a new home at 1 Devonshire Terrace, where they would remain for eleven years. Charles Dickens presided over an ever-growing family, augmented by the birth of Kate (Katie) Macready on October 29, 1839. She soon became her father's favorite child because she displayed more of Dickens's temperament, energy, and personality than did the other children. He gave her a special nickname, Lucifer's Box, because of

The Dickens home at 1 Devonshire Terrace.

her hot temper. Catherine continued to suffer poor health after the birth of each child. Their relationship remained complicated—Dickens could be cold and then passionately attentive, depending on his mood. As his children grew older, each noticed a distinct falling off in their father's affections. He preferred them to be small children, just as he seemed to prefer his wife to be an idea instead of a reality.

Though he had a growing family of his own to support, Dickens was still not free of his father's debts. After paying off yet another, he wrote to John Forster, "And so it always is, directly I build up a hundred pounds, one of my dear relations comes and knocks it down again."

In addition to the debts he owed various vendors, John Dickens had used his son's name to borrow from friends and acquaintances. For quite a while he hid the schemes from Charles's knowledge, but even the borrowed amounts were not enough to pay all of John's debts. Finally, Charles decided to remove his father from the temptations of London by renting a cottage outside the city for his parents and his youngest brother, Augustus. Dickens paid off some of his father's debts, then purchased the house and all its furnishings himself and sent his father, his mother, and brother away as though they were going on vacation. Still, his mother wrote complaining letters all summer. Dickens finally told Forster: "I do swear that I am sick at heart with both her and father too, and think this *is* too much."

Dickens's increasing fame brought requests for financial assistance from all manner of people. What few of them realized was that the famous author was hardly a millionaire. The lack of a strong copyright law meant what should have been copyrighted material was routinely stolen and reprinted without his permission. Dickens, frustrated by the financial loss, tried various schemes to protect his work but eventually had to resign himself to losing that money.

Once *Oliver Twist* had finished appearing in serial form, it was bound and released as a novel. Dickens spent time revising the work before it was published as a whole, smoothing out any sections that hinted at its original serialization and making other changes. He wrote quickly—sometimes more than 2,500 words a day—and did not often get to revise his work before it was serialized. His attitude towards previously published pieces changed over time—for a while, he could hardly stand to have the *Pickwick Papers* mentioned. It's likely he was to some degree frustrated by *Pickwick's* fame and regretted that later works were compared (sometimes unfavorably) to it.

In February, Dickens quarreled with Richard Bentley and quit editing the magazine. He decided to start a periodical of his own, one that would be produced weekly and would replicate the feel of the magazines he had cherished as a child. *Bentley's Miscellany* was a fashionable, in-the-know production. Dickens wanted something more reminiscent of his childhood. Though he was still writing *Nicholas Nickleby,* Dickens approached Chapman and Hall about the new project. Showing his increased skill as a negotiator, Dickens asked his publishers to fund the project and pay him a salary as well as a percentage of the profits. After receiving their go-ahead, he began work on *Master Humphrey's Clock.*

In February, Dickens and John Forster went to Bath, where they met Walter Savage Landor, an aging poet and essayist Dickens admired. Dickens's increasing fame led to an ever-growing circle of acquaintances and admirers, including some of the most important literary figures of the day.

It was during this visit that Dickens first visualized the character of Little Nell and conceived the idea for what would become *The Old Curiosity Shop.* At first, he planned her story to be just one of several in the new magazine. The first issue, with the Little Nell story, sold 70,000 copies, but sales dropped dramatically when the

The actual London antique shop on which Little Nell's story was based. (Library of Congress)

public realized that the story was not the start of a new novel. Dickens decided to turn the story of Little Nell into a weekly serial.

Little Nell, a pure, innocent girl, lives in an antique shop with her gambling grandfather, who owes money to an evil dwarf, Daniel Quilp. To escape this monster, Little Nell and her grandfather wander lost through the streets of London. Dickens soon realized that Little Nell was as compelling a character as Oliver Twist.

From the beginning, Dickens knew that the innocent Little Nell would die. A person as pure as she could only come to harm in a world filled with evil. Her death would not be unrealistic. In 1839, half of the funerals in London were for children under ten.

The weekly episodes about Little Nell were more

An illustration of Nell and her grandfather by George Cattermole for The Old Curiosity Shop. (Dickens House Museum, London)

popular than any of Dickens's previous novels. Each issue sold more than 100,000 copies. Readers became so caught up in Nell's story that Americans lined the New York piers waiting for the arrival of newspapers containing the next installment.

When the time came, Dickens had trouble writing Little Nell's death scene. He had come to identify her with his memories of his sister-in-law, Mary Hogarth. As he wrote to John Forster, "Old wounds bleed afresh." When he finished the novel, he declared, "Nobody will miss her [Little Nell] like I shall." Little Nell's death was also difficult for Dickens's readers—he was deluged by letters begging him to spare her life.

Dickens returned to Broadstairs, where he could work

Broadstairs, Dickens's favorite resort spot, located near Kent on England's eastern coast.

in relative peace. He kept to the same strict schedule he had maintained for years, writing every day from about 8:30 to two o'clock. He relaxed in the afternoons, often taking his customary long walks, then enjoyed having company with dinner. In an unusual move, he bought out the remainder of his contract with Richard Bentley, leaving him free of obligations. He continued to be as interested in human behavior as ever, always watching those around him. He was not a tall man, but he dressed sharply, usually wearing bright colors.

In the coming months, Dickens would return to a book that had languished through contractual disputes. *Barnaby Rudge* was the first of Dickens's two historical novels and deals with the Gordon riots of 1780, in which a mob of over a thousand people held London captive for a week, burning and ransacking public buildings. At issue was the lack of rights for Catholics. Dickens's nineteenth-century readers saw parallels between those riots and the Chartist Movement of their own time.

The Chartists, whose name derived from the People's Charter, demanded several election reforms, including voting rights for all men without property qualifications. They held large public meetings, and their clashes with authority led many British citizens to fear that riots like those of 1780 would erupt again in London.

Barnaby Rudge was the least popular of Dickens's

⅋ POLITICS AND PHILOSOPHY ⅋

Dickens's politics were often reflected in his novels. He was a strong advocate of reform and took a stance on most of the major social issues of the day. However, he was skeptical of the then-popular philosophy of Benthamism, which was based on the teachings and writings of Jeremy Bentham (1748-1832). Bentham, a lawyer who devoted his life to philosophy, argued that the desire to create the greatest amount of happiness for the greatest number of people should be the basis for making morally sound decisions. Dickens was not troubled by the idea of creating a more equitable society, but he was concerned that Bentham's philosophy did not give enough importance to the individual. Dickens believed that the greatest evil of industrialization was that it reduced the individual to a cog in a machine. Humans ran the risk of becoming economic units, not individual members of the human family. Dickens did, however, admire Bentham's commitment to reforming the legal system.

Another philosopher Dickens admired was Thomas Carlyle (1795-1881), a Scottish intellectual who rejected the materialism of the era and believed society could only be changed by great men, whom he called heroes. Carlyle's ideas influenced Dickens's writings, particularly his novel *Hard Times*, as well as his political beliefs. Carlyle himself enjoyed Dickens's work, although he discounted the value of fiction because he said it was too bound up with the world of appearances, which he rejected.

In some ways, Dickens resembled one of Carlyle's admired heroic figures. He was a striver, always on the edge, who did not shy away from criticizing political and social conditions. His love and compassion led him to regard Victorian England with the same awe and fear as Carlyle did, and they were both concerned that Great Britain was becoming nothing but an industrial wasteland.

serials. Sales plunged from 70,000 for the first installment to 3,000 by the last one. Dickens attributed the drop to his having saturated the market with five novels in five years. Critics cite the book's emphasis on history and mob psychology along with too many plot threads not carefully woven together. Whatever the reason for the book's unpopularity, Gabriel Varden's flirtatious daughter captured readers' hearts. She was Dickens's first portrayal of a pretty, lively young woman. Her colorful style of dress inspired the "Dolly Varden" look— a green chintz skirt with pink polka dots, divided in the front and pulled back to reveal a bright silk petticoat. Charles Dickens and his characters were becoming institutions—and he was not yet thirty years old.

On October 20, 1841, Dickens's twenty-year-old

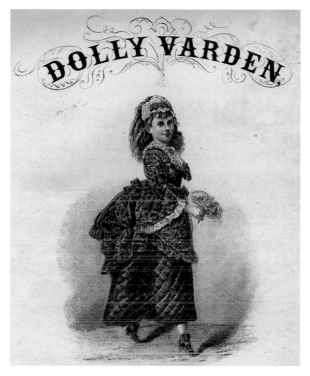

This mid-nineteenth-century print is an example of Dolly Varden fashion.
(Library of Congress)

brother-in-law, George Thomson Hogarth, died suddenly. Although Dickens allowed the young man's body
to be buried beside Mary Hogarth in the spot that Dickens
had previously reserved for himself, the decision did not
come easily. Dickens wrote to his friend John Forster, "It
is a great trial to me to give up Mary's grave, greater than
I can possibly express. . . . The desire to be buried next to
her is as strong upon me now as it was five years ago; and
I know . . . that it will never diminish."

Forster recognized the emotional strain his friend
was under and arranged with Chapman and Hall to make
an exception to Dickens's contract to give him a year

free from novel writing. *Master Humphrey's Clock* was proving to be an expensive publication, and Chapman and Hall were anxious for another novel to offset their losses. They realized, however, that Dickens was best handled with care and so agreed to the break. Still, the extra time away meant that Dickens would owe them even more when he returned to work. The young novelist was acutely aware of how many people depended on him and his talent.

Dickens had long been fascinated by the United States, which he believed exhibited the liberty, democracy, and lack of class distinctions that he wanted Great Britain to embrace. Dickens had exchanged several letters with the American writer Washington Irving, who encouraged him to come to the United States. In the correspondence, Irving told Dickens that if he came to America, "it would be a triumph for [him] . . . from one end of the States to the other, as was never known in any nation."

The more he thought about traveling to the United States during this break from writing, the more Dickens wanted to go. He wanted Catherine to accompany him on the six-month-long journey but knew it would be too much for the children. Dickens rented a house near the home of William Macready, his actor friend, and moved the children there, along with his brother Fred. Catherine had such a hard time with separation from the children that her fifteen-year-old sister, Georgina, promised to help take care of them.

In January 1842, the Dickenses boarded the steam-

Charles and Catherine Dickens took this 1842 painting of their children with them on their trip to America.

boat *Britannia* for Boston, Massachusetts. After surviving a stormy voyage, they received a warm welcome from large crowds in Boston that amazed and excited Dickens. He wrote to Forster, "How can I give you the faintest notion of my reception here; of the crowds that pour in and out the whole day; of the people that line the streets when I go out; of the cheering when I went to the theatre; of the copies of verses, letters of congratulation, welcomes of all kinds, balls, dinners, assemblies without end?"

Although he thrived on the attention for about a month, Dickens soon tired of the dinners, dances, and trips to the theater. He started refusing public appearances. Instead he enjoyed private visits with American writers like Irving, Henry Wadsworth Longfellow, and Edgar Allan Poe.

The steamship Britannia, *which transported the Dickenses to America in 1842.*

Though Dickens was glad to meet the writers he had heard so much about, he was disgusted by some American practices, especially spitting. Dickens grumbled publicly about American manners, food service, and overheated homes. But the criticism that riled Americans most concerned international copyright law. In the United States, foreign authors had no protection for their works, which were widely printed without compensation to the authors. Newspapers serialized his books at no cost to themselves while greatly increasing profits. For Charles Dickens, this involved millions of copies of his books. Throughout his United States tour, Dickens spoke out frequently and strongly about the need for a protective law. Soon there was a backlash, and Dickens was vilified as greedy.

Dickens and his wife traveled as far south as Richmond, Virginia, where slavery horrified them. On their train, in the car for blacks, was a female slave with her children. They were being separated from their husband

and father, who would remain a plantation slave while the wife and children were sold. The children cried the entire trip. On board a steamer, Dickens briefly talked to two constables and a slave owner searching for slaves who had run away that day. When the steamer passed under a weak bridge, Dickens noticed a posted sign listing the fines for driving too fast over its rotten boards. The fine for a white man was five dollars; for a slave, fifteen lashes with a whip. In a letter to John Forster, Dickens wrote that as he traveled out of the South, he was glad to turn his back on such an evil system: "I really don't think I could have borne it any longer."

Before returning home, the Dickenses saw parts of what was then the western United States, traveling as far west as St. Louis, Missouri. No matter where or how far he traveled, Dickens wrote each day, sometimes as many as 8,000 words, mostly letters to John Forster and other friends. When he returned home, he planned to retrieve the letters for use in *American Notes,* a book that would chronicle his travels.

One interesting benefit of Dickens's trip to America was that it broadened his thinking about the effects of the Industrial Revolution. Having seen the well-run mills of Massachusetts, he posited that it might not be the factories themselves that were evil, just the way in which they were managed.

The Dickenses arrived back in England in June, much to the joy of their children. Since the children had grown

Dickens wrote favorably of the working conditions in American mill towns, like Lowell, Massachusetts, a vibrant textile manufacturing center on the Merrimack River. (Library of Congress)

close to their Aunt Georgina during their parents' absence, she moved in with the family permanently. She, like her older sister Mary, adored Dickens. It was a happy time for the family.

By January 1843, Dickens had not published a novel in more than a year. His next venture, *The Life and Adventures of Martin Chuzzlewit,* began with disappointing sales. Dickens was determined to win his readers back and took advantage of the serial form to do so. He made an abrupt change in the plot and sent young Martin Chuzzlewit to America on a journey of self-discovery. All of his previous characters had retained their same traits throughout the entire story. Martin Chuzzlewit, in contrast, metamorphoses from an immature, self-centered youth to someone who cares for other people.

Although Dickens and his publishers, Chapman and

Hall, argued about this plot change, the character's excursion to the United States boosted sales while giving Dickens one more chance to point out some of the things that most irritated him about Americans. He was pleased with the novel and wrote to John Forster, "I think *Chuzzlewit* in a hundred points immeasurably the best of my stories. . . . I feel my power now, more than I ever did . . . I have greater confidence in myself than I have ever had." Readers did not seem to agree, as sales never reached more than 23,000 for any single episode—good numbers for any other author, but a serious drop-off for Dickens.

In February 1843, John Dickens was back in the city, having failed to keep up the lease on the cottage outside London. Despite the allowance that Charles sent him, the elder Dickens could not manage to stay out of debt. John tried to get some of his creditors to back off by offering them pages from a farce that Dickens had written for the family's entertainment. An irritated Charles wrote to a friend, "The thought of [John Dickens] besets me, night and day, and I really do not know what is to be done with him. It is quite clear that the more we do, the more outrageous and audacious he becomes."

One of Dickens's chief concerns was young criminals. Unwanted and abandoned children filled London's streets. They had no one to teach them right and wrong, and circumstances forced them into lives of crime. When caught breaking the law, they were thrown into prisons with adult criminals. Dickens believed that the only way to break this cycle was universal education: "If you would reward honesty, if you would give encouragement to good, if you would stimulate the idle, eradicate evil, or correct what is bad, education . . . is the one thing needful, and the one effective end."

Angela Burdett-Coutts.

Angela Burdett-Coutts, a wealthy philanthropist, asked Dickens to help her evaluate some potential charities. Knowing his interest in education, she asked him to visit Field Lane School, one of the so-called "Ragged Schools" that had developed to educate poor children living in the slums. John Pounds, a Portsmouth shoemaker, had started the first Ragged School in 1818. In 1844, Anthony Ashley Cooper, Earl of Shaftesbury, formed the Ragged School Union. Under his forty-year chairmanship, over 300,000 poor children received a free education.

The Ragged Schools found an ally in Dickens. His

frequent visits and his firsthand knowledge of the problems they faced made him a useful advisor to Burdett-Coutts. After Dickens made a visit to the Field Lane School, he wrote that it was "held in three most wretched rooms on the first floor of a rotten house . . . there is no such thing as dress among the seventy pupils; certainly not . . . a whole suit of clothes, among them all. I have very seldom seen, in all the strange and dreadful things I have seen in London and elsewhere, anything so shocking as the dire neglect of soul and body exhibited among these children."

Despite the drab environment, Dickens praised the work of the teachers, who treated the boys kindly. The students readily answered both Dickens's and the schoolmaster's questions. Dickens recommended any financial aid that Burdett-Coutts could give—especially any that would improve sanitation. Though Dickens was still writing furiously, he also found time to contribute to making England a better place to live, especially for the children of the working class—children like the one he had been.

In December, Dickens published the first of five Christmas stories, *A Christmas Carol,* which has become his most famous work. Facing increasing financial pressures and the lukewarm reception of his last two books, Dickens hoped a Christmas story would bring in additional money. He and his publishers Chapman and Hall were still at odds. They agreed to publish the book only if Dickens paid the costs.

Dickens wanted a high-quality Christmas book, so he

had the small book bound in red cloth with a gold design on the front and on the spine. The edges of the pages were trimmed in gold. *Punch* magazine artist John Leech contributed eight illustrations, four of them hand-colored. Dickens priced the book at a relatively inexpensive five shillings. The book sold 6,000 copies in the first few days and 15,000 copies by the end of 1844. However, because of the high publication costs, the profit margin was smaller.

A Christmas Carol tells the story of the miserly Ebenezer Scrooge, a selfish old man who is visited by the ghost of his old business partner and then by the ghosts of Christmases past, present, and future. Given the opportunity to see himself and his life from an outsider's perspective, Scrooge comes to realize and regret that he has devoted himself to making money at the expense of the happiness of those around him. In the end, he seizes an opportunity to redeem himself. From a miser who is "a squeezing, wrenching, grasping, scraping, clutching, covetous old sinner," Scrooge becomes a changed man, "an angel . . . as merry as a schoolboy." He opens his heart—and his wallet—to help the family of his employee, Bob Cratchit, and in particular Cratchit's son, Tiny Tim.

The book took Dickens only six weeks to write. Though he wrote quickly, he took immense care and *A Christmas Carol,* like his other works, has stood the test of time. *A Christmas Carol* reminds readers that money cannot buy happiness—a lesson Dickens had learned many times over.

Scrooge's third Visitor

This illustration by John Leech was made for A Christmas Carol *in 1843.* (Victoria & Albert Museum, London)

Dickens felt immense economic pressure from all sides. Not only was he the sole support for his own large family, but members of his extended family—especially his father and his brothers—depended on him as well. Dickens was always aware of the sales figures of his latest books. He worried that when Chapman and Hall asked for another book they were disregarding the possibility he had saturated the market. The pressure made Dickens want to disappear. He negotiated his way out of the Chapman and Hall contract, packed up his family—which now included their fifth child, Francis Jeffrey (Frank) Dickens—and headed to mainland Europe.

Living expenses in Italy were much cheaper than in London. In Genoa, Dickens found Bella Vista, a palazzo which could accommodate his entire family—twelve people, including the servants. Before leaving London, Dickens signed a contract with new publishers, Bradbury and Evans, who produced the popular magazine *Punch*. They offered Dickens a large advance for another Christmas book.

Dickens was happy in Italy. He continued to write, determined to fulfill the terms of the Bradbury and Evans contract. He took his customary long walks, this time soaking up the new sights and sounds, and enjoyed the increased privacy he found outside his native country. He spent a year abroad, and in many ways it was exactly what he needed.

While in Italy, Dickens completed his second Christmas story, *The Chimes*. He was extremely proud of the finished manuscript and could hardly wait to get back to England to show it to his friends and publishers. Leaving the family in Genoa he hurried to London, where he offered a series of private readings. He was greatly moved by the experience and would continue to

Dickens giving a reading of The Chimes *to a group of his friends in Forster's apartment at Lincoln's Inn Fields in London.*

dramatize his stories for the rest of his life. Dickens often spoke the words of his compositions out loud as he wrote and had taken roles in his own plays, but this was the first time he had experimented with reading his prose aloud and was amazed at the effect it had on him and his readers.

In July 1845, with Catherine again pregnant, Dickens moved the family back to England. On October 28, the Dickenses' sixth child, Alfred D'Orsay Tennyson Dickens, was born. Dickens nicknamed this tiny baby with the long name "Skittles." Catherine's health continued to suffer from her pregnancies, and their marriage did not bear the strain well. Dickens even became infatuated with a young woman he met at a reading, and while nothing came of his feelings for her, it was a sign of the deteriorating state of his marriage. The woman, Christiana Weller, he wrote to a friend, reminded him very much of Mary Hogarth.

In December 1845, Bradbury and Evans published

Catherine Dickens in 1846.

Dickens's third Christmas book, *The Cricket on the Hearth*. Dickens started a newspaper, the *Daily News,* and became its editor. John Forster advised Dickens not to get involved in the newspaper business, fearing that it would take time away from his novels. Dickens ignored his advice and threw himself into the work. He hired a staff that probably included his own father as a reporter, and oversaw nearly every aspect of preparing the paper for publication. The first issue appeared on January 21, 1846.

The paper addressed many of the important issues of the time. The mid-1840s was a tumultuous period in European history. Widespread social unrest would eventually lead to a series of revolutions over most of the continent in 1848. The beginning of the Irish Potato Famine was already increasing tensions in that country.

The demands made by the People's Charter had mostly gone unmet, though there were some signs that Parliament understood the need for reform. The hated Corn Laws, which had artificially inflated the price of grain and thus raised expenditures for every citizen in order to protect landowners, were repealed in 1846.

Dickens's time spent editing the *Daily News* was short, however. As much as he enjoyed having an impact on Victorian society and politics through journalism, he soon discovered he was not temperamentally suited to work with the paper's editorial staff. He resigned only nineteen days after the first issue appeared.

There was another reason to get out of the newspaper business. Although he had written the three Christmas stories, as well as *Pictures from Italy,* a book about his travels, Dickens had not written a novel for two years. He was anxious to get back to a longer writing project. It was time to prove he could still hold the public's interest over an extended period of time.

As usual, Dickens was involved in several projects. It was not easy to extricate himself from the newspaper and he had a heavy speaking schedule. He was also working closely with Angela Burdett-Coutts on a major charitable undertaking. Urania Cottage was a rehabilitation center for prostitutes, female ex-prisoners, and homeless mothers. Dickens found a house in Shepherd's Bush to use for the cottage and became deeply involved in the project. No detail was too small for him. He selected the first group of women to live at Urania

Cottage and decided on their daily schedule, their training course, and even the fabric for their dresses.

Dickens decided it was time to leave England again.
This time he rented a villa in Lausanne, Switzerland,
where he hoped to find the peace and quiet he needed
to write a novel. But it could not be too perfect. He
needed a certain amount of tumult to fire up his imagination. The right balance of quiet and chaos was getting
harder and harder to find.

Four

Changing Times

O nce settled at the villa in Lausanne, Dickens
tried to begin serious work on the new novel,
Dombey and Son. The ideas did not come
easily. He missed his walks around London and could
not concentrate on one book. His mind darted from one
idea to the next. Finally, he settled down and planned out
each stage of the story.

Modern critics see *Dombey and Son* as a turning
point in Dickens's fiction. In it he dealt with Victorian
society as a whole rather than with a specific social
issue. *Dombey and Son* explores women's roles in the
rapidly changing world and the place of the railroad in
nineteenth-century England. More tightly structured
than his earlier novels, it has a unity of action and theme
not previously seen.

Dickens's new publishers, Bradbury and Evans, whetted readers' appetites for the forthcoming serial with an extensive publicity campaign. The first installment's sales of 25,000 copies rewarded their efforts, and Dickens felt certain that it was going to be a success. He wrote John Forster: "If any of my books are read years hence, *Dombey* will be remembered as among the best of them."

In gratitude for Dickens's assistance with Urania Cottage, Burdett-Coutts offered to pay for Charley to attend Eton. Dickens was quick to accept. On April 18, 1847, Catherine gave birth to the couple's seventh child, Sydney Smith Haldimand Dickens. Catherine had an especially difficult time with this birth; eight months later she suffered another miscarriage.

Dickens formed an amateur acting company and, serving as actor-manager, began rehearsals of Ben Jonson's *Every Man in His Humour.* He planned to use the proceeds from the eight performances to purchase and preserve William Shakespeare's birthplace at Stratford-on-Avon. Dickens played the lead role, and the performances received favorable reviews from the London *Times.*

In 1847, William Makepeace Thackeray began the serialization of *Vanity Fair,* a novel that critics quickly compared to those of Dickens. *Vanity Fair* was serialized at the same time *Dombey and Sons* was appearing. However, the authors represented two different views of society and of human nature. Dickens entertained his readers with plots full of surprising changes of fortune, caricatures, and exaggeration. He wanted people to

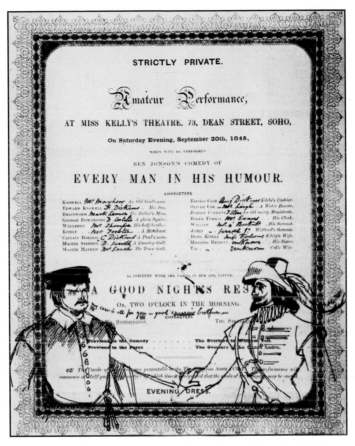

The playbill for Dickens's 1845 production of Every Man in His Humour.

react with emotion to his writings. Thackeray, on the other hand, presented a more realistic view of life. He was more interested in his characters' interactions with one another than with the public's reaction to the characters. He seemed more tolerant of humanity's failings than Dickens was. Thackeray saw mankind's shortcomings as the result of the good and evil present in the human condition. Dickens was more likely to try to place blame on individuals.

William Makepeace Thackeray. (Library of Congress)

Both men were members of the Garrick Club, a London social club. They were not close, although each admired the other's work. The rivalry for readers and royalties was more on Thackeray's part than Dickens's. Thackeray was proud of *Vanity Fair* and, after a year of its serialization, wrote to his mother that he was "all but at the top of the tree . . . having a great fight up there with Dickens."

Dickens had more problems to occupy his thoughts than competition with Thackeray. Throughout July, he spent time with his older sister, Fanny Burnett. She was dying. He tried to comfort Fanny, who worried about her children, especially her son, Henry Jr., the model for Tiny Tim in *A Christmas Carol.* Dickens vowed to do all he could to help.

As Fanny lingered, Dickens went for a brief visit to Broadstairs, where Catherine and the children were vacationing. Near the end of August, he received word that Fanny had only a few days left. Dickens rushed to her bedside before she died on

September 2. John Forster helped Dickens with the funeral arrangements. Fanny was buried at Highgate Cemetery; a year later they buried her son Henry beside her.

That December, Dickens published the last of his five Christmas books, *The Haunted Man and the Ghost's Bargain.* In January, Catherine gave birth to Henry Fielding Dickens. Dickens hoped that Henry, their eighth child, would be their last. Catherine's health remained poor, and his growing family was a financial drain.

Fanny's death brought back Dickens's childhood memories, especially those unhappy ones of his father's imprisonment at Marshalsea and his work at Warren's Blacking Factory. Then John Forster unwittingly brought these issues out into the open. A mutual friend told Forster that he remembered seeing Dickens working at Warren's when he was a boy. Forster asked Dickens about it—before this Dickens had never discussed that time with anyone.

Dickens wrote a brief autobiographical sketch about that period of his life. He showed the memoir to Forster. When Dickens confided to Forster that he would like to share the story but did not want to write an autobiography, Forster suggested incorporating it into a first-person narrative. Dickens liked the idea.

About this same time Dickens was writing a series of articles for the *Examiner* on the abuse of orphan children. From these two interests, the article and his autobiography, Dickens conceived the character David

Copperfield, a fatherless boy who later loses his mother.

Excited about the new idea, Dickens set up a concentrated writing schedule. He worked slowly, still unsure where he planned to take the story. By the fifth installment, he began to write faster, using details of his own childhood and youth.

The novel is full of autobiographical elements. David's first trip to the theater is just like Dicken's; he goes to work at Murdstone and Grinby's, a stand-in for Warren's; his love for Dora Spenlow reflects Dickens's infatuation with Maria Beadnell. David even learns shorthand to become a reporter.

As he worked on *David Copperfield,* Dickens moved his family back to London, where he continued to supervise activities at Urania Cottage as well as to begin plans for a new weekly magazine. He needed the latter to supplement his income when the first three installments of *David Copperfield* did not sell as well as he had hoped. Dickens finished the novel in October and wrote to Forster: "If I were to say half of what *Copperfield* makes me feel to-night . . . I would be turned inside-out."

Dickens considered *David Copperfield* his best work, and despite somewhat slower initial sales, it was a favorite of his readers. One critic proclaimed it "the best of all the author's fictions." The novel focused on Dickens's own journey of self-discovery. He structured it around the use of memory as a means of bringing a person to self-understanding.

The character David Copperfield is an orphan, aban-

An illustration by Phiz for David Copperfield. (Courtesy of Art Resource.)

doned by his family. Dickens may have secretly longed to share this condition—his own family continued to be a burden. His brother Fred, whose marriage was failing and who continued to pile up debts as he moved from job to job, used Dickens's name to borrow money. Once again, his family exaggerated how wealthy he was. Dickens wasn't the millionaire they apparently thought him to be. He was making substantial sums of money, but it went out even faster than it came in.

In August 1850, Catherine gave birth to their ninth child, Dora Annie Dickens, named to recall David Copperfield's young bride, Dora Spenlow. Although he would have preferred no more children, Dickens was glad a daughter had broken the succession of sons. Because of his busy schedule and his wife's poor health, Dora Annie was mostly cared for by servants. She was not a strong baby, and eight months later, John Forster had to inform Dickens that his little girl had gone into convulsions and died. Just a few months later, John Dickens died during a painful operation for which he received no anesthesia. Dickens was with his father when he died and promised that he would take care of his mother. Then, for the last time, he paid off his father's debts.

Dickens was now nearing forty and unquestionably the preeminent writer of his time. He was in great demand as a speaker and thoroughly enjoyed every opportunity he had to dramatize his works. Still, he was not ready to rest on his laurels.

Dickens's publishers, Bradbury and Evans, agreed to publish his new weekly magazine, *Household Words,* even though Dickens demanded a 50 percent share in the paper and complete control over its content. He hired W. H. Wills as his assistant.

Dickens wanted the magazine to cover a wide variety of subjects, from commentary on social abuses to fiction. Its primary audience was the middle class, a group

Dickens continued to have great sympathy for. He envisioned the magazine would offer hope and enlightenment to its readers, many of whom struggled to survive. Dickens oversaw every detail of the magazine. The first issue sold over 100,000 copies, and Dickens was delighted with the profits.

Although Dickens resented the frequent demands for money from family members, he was generous with other people. Hoping to raise funds to provide pensions and housing for struggling writers, he enlisted the aid of novelist Edward Bulwer-Lytton, who wrote a comic play called *Not so Bad as We Seem*. Dickens took the lead role and wanted his assistant editor to take a part as well. When Wills refused to do so, Dickens secured the services of Wilkie Collins, a young writer just making himself known. Although Dickens was twelve years older than Collins, the two became close friends.

The play, performances of which were by invitation only, was the talk of London. Even Queen Victoria requested tickets, though her mentor, Prime Minister Lord Melbourne, had advised her against reading Dickens's books. But the queen was no longer the naïve eighteen-year-old who had assumed the throne fourteen years before. She and her husband, Prince Albert, were interested in England's social problems. They supported several charities that helped the poor. Because Victoria was a constitutional monarch, she had limited powers over Parliament, but she still had a significant influence over the hearts and minds of the English people. Her presence at the theater implied her support for Dickens's charitable endeavor—a weighty endorsement.

That summer, Dickens leased Tavistock House, even though it was "in the dirtiest of all possible conditions." But the house was large enough to accommodate his family and after significant remodeling and renovations "might be made very handsome." Charley, now fourteen, entered Eton to study for a career in merchant banking. Angela Burdett-Coutts paid his fees as promised.

By November, Tavistock House was ready for occupancy, and the Dickens family, along with his sister-in-

Tavistock House in London, home of the Dickenses from 1851 through 1860.

law Georgina, moved in. On March 13, 1852, Catherine gave birth at home to Edward Bulwer Lytton Dickens. This seventh son and tenth child was their last. As the baby of the family, Edward eventually became his father's pet, nicknamed "Plorn," but at his birth Dickens commented, "My wife has presented me with No. 10. I think I could have dispensed with the compliment."

Dickens was heavily committed to charitable works, public speeches, amateur theatricals, and editing *Household Words*. He had just suffered the deaths of his father and infant daughter, and had to contend with Catherine's continued illness. Yet he began to feel the nervousness that always preceded the start of a new story, and soon *Bleak House* was born.

Bleak House was the first in a series of social novels. Long and complex, it centers around a court case and highlights Dickens's disdain for England's slow-moving legal system. *Little Dorrit*, written soon after *Bleak House*, put the British prison system and England's class system under the same scrutiny.

Even though he had many demands for his time and attention, Dickens followed his strict writing schedule. Eventually, the pressure caused him to succumb to the recurring illness of his childhood, the severe pain in his side caused by his kidney ailment. Dickens spent a week in bed and an additional few days convalescing.

In October 1853, in search of a needed break from the pressure, Dickens went on a European trip with Wilkie Collins and another friend. They had no set itinerary, and

The eldest of the Dickens children, Charley, in 1851.

Dickens was able to relax completely. Collins reminded Dickens of the fun he had had in his bachelor days—or perhaps of the fun he could have enjoyed more if he had not been so concerned about earning money. Dickens had missed much of his youth because he drove himself so fiercely, yet he expected the same effort from his own children. Dickens and his friends met Charley in Paris, where Charley informed his father that he had left Eton. Although he had made some progress in his studies, he had not applied himself enough to succeed.

Dickens was disappointed in his oldest son. He had high hopes for each of his sons and expected them to follow his rules and advice. Charley and his brothers had all grown up with an anxious desire to please their father and a lack of self-confidence because they could not seem to do so. The affection he had lavished on them as children turned to indifference as they aged, leaving them confused and unhappy. He admitted to having a "habit of suppression . . . which makes me chary of showing my affection, even to my children, except when they are very young." Charley was the first to experience this bewildering withdrawal of his father's love. The rest would soon learn how it felt.

In early 1854, declining subscriptions forced Dickens to add a serialization of a novel to *Household Words*. He gave the magazine his newest work, *Hard Times*. The story describes a family who suffers the dehumanizing effects of Britain's industrialization. He uses their experiences to show readers how individuals can be lost within a system. But Dickens was not just a social critic—he was foremost a storyteller who cared for his characters and created realistic and engaging worlds for them to inhabit. At the same time he wanted his readers to see their world through more critical eyes.

To learn more about the relationship between owners and employees, Dickens traveled to Preston, where a weavers' strike had lasted twenty-nine weeks. He did not stay long in Preston but gathered enough material for an article in *Household Words* that conveyed his belief that in all of life's relationships, including those between employees and employers, there must be mutual respect and consideration.

By the last episode of *Hard Times,* circulation of *Household Words* had quadrupled. Critics received the book with mixed feelings, however. Thomas Ruskin, a writer who shared many of Dickens's views, thought *Hard Times* was one of Dickens's finest novels. Others

---

◌ DICKENS AND THE CRITICS ◌

Most of Dickens's books were immediately popular with his readership. His vivid portrayals of life in Victorian England won him legions of faithful fans, and his affection for the common man endeared him to an audience that cut across class distinctions. Occasionally, he was taken to task for being overly sentimental, as in the case of Little Nell's death in *The Old Curiosity Shop.* Yet sentimentality also characterizes some of his best-loved works, such as *A Christmas Carol.*

Dickens used the serial format shrewdly, ending each install-ment with a cliffhanger guaranteed to leave readers wanting more. He was also willing to adjust his plots in accordance with popular reaction to previous installments.

Dickens's influence on future generations of writers is immea-surable. Most of his novels are still in print, and many have been adapted for the stage or made into movies. Dickens's portraits of Britain in the 1800s have shaped modern-day perceptions of the Victorian era. Though he was not a realist writer, he still conveyed a sense of the grittiness of the times. The list of writers crediting Dickens as an inspiration is far too long to name them all, but includes Russian writers Ivan Turgenev and Feodor Dostoyevsky, the Americans Washington Irving and Mark Twain, and modern figures such as George Orwell and J. K. Rowling.

---

saw it merely as a statement of Dickens's political views. One critic called it a dull, disappointing melodrama.

After finishing this book, Dickens still maintained a busy writing and public-reading schedule. He had achieved great renown as a novelist but was still not satisfied. He continued to walk the streets of London seeking new inspiration for more books.

Dickens's restlessness got a jolt when, in 1855, he received a letter from Maria Beadnell, the woman he had loved as a young man. She was now Maria Beadnell Winter, married with a family of her own. The contents of her first letter to Dickens are lost, but they quickly entered into a flurry of correspondence that culminated in the arrangement of a semi-secret meeting.

Dickens was over forty now, and Maria two years older, but Dickens seemed to believe he was going to meet the woman he had loved and lost more than twenty years before. He was horrified to discover she was now plump and middle-aged. He

Maria Beadnell Winter as an older woman.

cut the meeting short and refused any further contact with her.

Dickens's disappointment in Maria reflected the way his feelings for his wife had changed. He was disillusioned with Catherine and, increasingly, with his children. Yet he clung to the belief that he could create the happy home he had lacked as a child.

That month, as Dickens celebrated his forty-third birthday, he was out for a walk when he saw that Gad's Hill Place was up for sale. This was the house John Dickens had pointed to as the kind of place Charles might someday own if he worked hard enough. Now, the adult Charles Dickens saw an opportunity to achieve one of his earliest dreams. He paid 1,700 pounds for the old house.

Five

Turning Points

❧

The Dickens family moved into Gad's Hill Place in 1857, after summering in France while renovations were completed. Charley, the Dickens's oldest son, remained in London with his maternal grandparents to work at Barings Bank.

In September, Dickens's friend Wilkie Collins joined the staff of *Household Words*. Over the summer, Dickens and Collins had written a melodrama, *The Frozen Deep*. When Dickens learned that an old friend had died suddenly, leaving a widow and children, he decided to hold several benefit performances of *The Frozen Deep* to raise money. Members of his own family and friends took most of the roles.

Audiences responded so favorably to the play that Dickens received an invitation to bring it to the Free

Ellen "Nelly" Ternan.

Trade Hall. He replaced his own daughters with professional actresses: Fanny Ternan and her two youngest daughters, Marie and Ellen. Dickens continued to play the lead male role.

Eighteen-year-old Ellen Ternan, called Nelly, was a petite, blue-eyed blonde. Dickens was quickly smitten with her. When the play finished and Mrs. Ternan took her children away to their next production, Dickens began planning a way to find Nelly again. He and Catherine were soon sleeping in separate bedrooms.

Dickens went on a walking tour with Wilkie Collins, supposedly to gather information for some new sketches. In reality he was hoping to see Nelly, who was performing in the Theatre Royal in Doncaster. Just before he left, he wrote to John Forster, "Poor Catherine and I are not made for each other, and there is no help for it. It is not only that she makes me uneasy and unhappy, but that I make her so too—and much more so . . . we are strangely ill-assorted for the bond there is between us. God knows she would have been a thousand times happier if she had married another kind of man . . . I am often cut to the heart by thinking what a pity it is, for her own sake, that I ever fell in her way."

Dickens's sympathy for his wife was short-lived. He began to make public statements about Catherine's shortcomings, suggesting that she was not a good mother and cared little about her children. His statements infuriated Catherine, but she found little support, even from her own family. Her sister, Georgina, seemed to side with Charles, and the children, torn between their hysterical mother and their calm, impenetrable father, generally sided with the latter.

Matters came to a head when a jeweler delivered to Catherine a bracelet Dickens intended for Nelly—clearly inscribed with her initials. When Catherine confronted him, Dickens flew into a rage, charging that her jealousy had gotten out of hand. He claimed that he always sent jewelry to his actresses after a performance.

Dickens forced Catherine to make a social call upon Nelly and her mother. Whether he wanted to stop rumors about the bracelet or whether he wanted to punish Catherine by making her look at her more youthful competition, no one knows. After bearing ten children in twenty years, Catherine was, as William Moy Thomas, a contributor to *Household Words,* described her, "a great fat lady—florid with arms thick as the leg of a Life Guard's man and as red as a beef sausage." As Catherine prepared for the visit, tears streamed down her face. Her daughter Kate demanded to know why her mother was crying. Catherine explained, "Your father has asked me to go and see Ellen Ternan." Kate tried to stop her from going.

Catherine's mother urged her daughter to leave Dickens. However, Victorian women did not leave their families, and Catherine's youngest child Edward was only six years old. Dickens wanted Catherine to say their parting was by mutual agreement. When she refused, he made plans for a separation in May 1858.

Catherine Dickens in 1857.

Dickens's friend Angela Burdett-Coutts tried to persuade him to stay with his wife. He wrote to her, "Nothing on earth—no, not even you—no consideration, human or Divine, can move me from the resolution I have taken."

Negotiations began. John Forster represented Dickens, and another old friend, Mark Lemon, an editor for *Punch*, represented Catherine. Although Dickens offered suggestions for how they could separate, Catherine refused any plan that caused her to live in the same house with him. In the final agreement, Catherine received her own house and an allowance of six hundred pounds a year. Her oldest son, Charley, went to live with her, but he wrote to his father: "Don't suppose that in making my choice, I was actuated by any feeling of preference for my mother to you. God knows I love you dearly, and it will be a hard day for me when I have to part from you and the girls. But in doing as I have done, I hope I am doing my duty, and that you will understand it so."

Dickens kept the other children with him. Although he did not forbid them to visit their mother, they seldom did. Years after her mother's death, Kate recalled, "We were all very wicked not to take her part."

Gossip about the Dickens's separation infuriated Charles. He forced Catherine's mother and her sister Helen to sign a statement withdrawing any negative comments they might have made about his character. When they hesitated, he threatened to cut off Catherine's allowance. They signed a retraction of their remarks, but Dickens still forbade his children to have any further contact with their grandmother or their aunt. He never saw Catherine again.

Dickens could certainly hold a grudge. When Charley married the daughter of a man he considered a traitorous friend, Dickens not only refused to attend the wedding but had his son's name stricken from consideration for acceptance to the Garrick Club.

The club caused additional trouble when Edmund Yates, who by now had become Dickens's protégé, published a critical article about William Makepeace Thackeray in *Town Talk*. Thackeray was furious, not only about the letter but because Yates had written a complimentary article about Dickens the previous month. Thackeray demanded an apology. Yates refused.

Thackeray decided that the only place that Yates could have obtained some of the information in the article was from conversations overheard at the Garrick Club.

Edmund Yates in 1858.

The club had a standing policy that nothing said inside its walls was repeated outside those rooms.

Thackeray asked for a hearing. Although the club voted seventy to forty-six that Yates should apologize personally to Thackeray, Dickens supported Yates's stand. When Yates refused to apologize, he was expelled. Thackeray was furious that Dickens had sided with Yates. The two argued and had no further contact until just a few weeks before Thackeray's death.

Against the advice of several friends, Dickens prepared an explanation of his and Catherine's separation, which he published in the June 12, 1858, edition of *Household Words.* In it he claimed the matter had been settled amicably. Because he feared the rumors had reached the United States, he sent a letter to the American agent who organized his reading tours. He told the agent to show it to influential people. When the contents appeared in the *New York Tribune,* Dickens exploded that the American had not used more discretion. From that time on, he referred to it as the "violated letter."

He sent the statement that had appeared in *Household Words* to other magazines, not realizing that most people cared little about his marriage problems. When Mark Lemon, Catherine's representative in the separation negotiations, refused to publish the letter in *Punch,* Dickens quarreled with him and the magazine's publishers, Bradbury and Evans. Because they stood firm, Dickens fired them as his publishers, stopped publication of *Household Words,* and went back to his former publishers, Chapman and Hall. The one person conspicuously absent during these proceedings was Nelly Ternan her-

An announcement for a reading by Dickens in Dublin during his 1858 tour.

self—her reaction to the scandal is unknown.

In the fall of 1858, Dickens began a highly acclaimed tour. He gave eighty-three readings in forty-four places throughout England. He loved to read and practiced in the mirror for hours on end. The tour's success invigorated him, and he planned a new weekly magazine to be called *All the Year Round.* As always, he knew the best way to insure sales of a periodical was to serialize a new story. Dickens began his twelfth book, the historical novel *A Tale of Two Cities,* to launch this new magazine.

Dickens had first conceived the idea for *A Tale of Two Cities* when he played the lead role in Wilkie Collins's drama *The Frozen Deep.* Dickens had performed the death scene of a man who had sacrificed his own life to save another—his rival for the woman he loved. On stage with him at the time was Nelly Ternan, playing the role

This cartoon of Dickens was inspired by the success of his magazine, All the Year Round. (Victoria & Albert Museum, London)

of a character named Lucy. Nelly became Dickens's model for Lucie Manette, a main character in *A Tale of Two Cities.*

As the story developed, other parallels to Dickens's life became evident. Lucie's father, Dr. Manette, had been imprisoned in the Bastille for the same number of years that Dickens was married. Just as Dr. Manette was freed from his shackles, Dickens had been freed from his marriage. It was as though the novel were meant to resolve all the problems of his life. Dickens wrote the episodes at a furious pace.

As Dickens wrote, he departed from the emphasis on character development that had made his work so popular. Consequently, critics have assessed many of the characters in *A Tale of Two Cities* as flat and hollow. The French Revolution served as the setting for the story's plot, and Dickens reflected the torment of his own life as he emphasized the horrors of the French Revolution—the mob, the sharpening of knives and axes, the tumbrels carrying victims to the guillotine. The action moves back and forth between London and Paris, much as Dickens alternately lived in the two cities. He made use of other pairs as well, the most famous of which is the look-alikes, Charles Darnay and Sydney Carton. In the end, Charles Darnay, who has the same initials as Charles Dickens, is saved, perhaps reflecting Dickens's hope that a happy ending was still possible for his own life.

Readers loved the story, and *All the Year Round's* circulation quickly grew to over 100,000 per issue. Although a few reviewers did praise A *Tale of Two Cities*, in general it has not been a favorite of critics. Most do not feel that it reached the literary level of his previous satires. The severest criticism charged that the novel was

Gad's Hill Place in 1860.

"a dish of puppy pie and stewed cat . . . not disguised by the cooking."

Dickens spent the summer with his children at Gad's Hill Place, where Catherine's sister Georgina served as his housekeeper and taught the younger boys to read before they were old enough to go to school. How Catherine felt about her unmarried sister continuing to live in Dickens's house is not known. However, many years later, in her will, all Catherine left to Georgina was a ring in the shape of a snake.

After a year at home with his mother, Charley went to Hong Kong to learn the tea trade for Barings Bank. He was out of England in 1860 when his sister married Charles Allston Collins, the younger brother of Wilkie

Kate Dickens Collins, shortly after her marriage.

Collins. Kate did not marry for love but rather out of a desire to get away from her tense home. She blamed her father for her parents' separation. Dickens knew Collins, an artist, because he worked on both *Household Words* and *All the Year Round*. Dickens strongly opposed Kate's marriage to the shy, moody young man, whom he did not believe was a good match for his hot-tempered, strong-willed daughter. Kate ignored her father's warnings and planned an elegant wedding for July 17 at Higham Parish Church, to be followed by an extravagant breakfast at Gad's Hill Place.

Despite being the mother of the bride, Catherine was not invited to the wedding or to the breakfast. Instead she sat in her own home, facing a clock, and imagined what was happening as each minute ticked by. After the breakfast, the couple left for a honeymoon in France and Belgium. That night, Mamie found her father in Kate's bedroom, the wedding dress clutched in his hands, as he knelt by Kate's bed and sobbed, "But for me, Katie would not have left home."

Only ten days later, Dickens suffered another loss with the death of his brother Alfred, who left behind a widow and five children. Although Dickens did not like his sister-in-law, he gave money to her and the children for the rest of his life. Near the end of July, Dickens sold Tavistock House—it was filled with too many memories—and moved permanently to Gad's Hill Place, where, in the garden, he built a small Swiss chalet sent to him in ninety-four pieces by a French friend. There he did most of his writing.

Still angry over the "violated letter," Dickens decided to burn all of the papers and letters he had accumulated over a twenty-year period. He did not want to leave behind any private documents. In his will, he would later write, "I rest my claims to the remembrance of my country upon my published works, and to remembrance of my friends upon their experience of me."

On September 3, in a field at Gad's Hill Place, Dickens started a bonfire. Two of his young sons, eight-year-old Plorn and eleven-year-old Henry, excitedly fed load after load of papers to the flames. When nothing remained but ashes, Dickens remarked, "Would to God every letter I had ever written was on that pile." Among the ashes were thousands of letters written to him by Wilkie Collins, Washington Irving, Thomas Carlyle, William Makepeace Thackeray, and Alfred Lord Tennyson.

Young Sydney Dickens in 1860 during his service in the Royal Navy as a midshipman.

Toward the end of the month, Dickens traveled to Portsmouth with his son Sydney, who had always loved the sea. Sydney had qualified for training as a naval officer. Again, Dickens bid farewell to one of his children, as thirteen-year-old Sydney departed to become a midshipman in the Royal Navy.

Dickens encouraged fifteen-year-old Alfred to take an engineering course so he could join the army. But Alfred failed the qualifying examination. Dickens then urged him to try for a career in the tea trade in India or China. He never quite knew what to do with sons who did not possess his enthusiasm, energy, or abilities. They, in turn, did not know how to please a father who demanded so much from them.

Dickens started work on his thirteenth novel, *Great Expectations,* which began serialization in *All the Year Round* in December. Sales of the magazine had dropped while serializing the work of another author. Dickens decided that to save the magazine's circulation, he needed to make *Great Expectations* a weekly serial instead of a monthly. Although he did not like weekly serials, he was willing to change the format in order to see a quicker boost in sales.

While trying to write an essay in a humorous style reminiscent of the *Pickwick Papers,* Dickens had conceived the idea of a story about a young boy named Pip. Consequently, he reread *David Copperfield* to avoid being repetitive. The stories did have similarities—they were both first person narratives about an orphan boy who grows up feeling unwanted and who has to struggle to survive. But the new character, Pip, became an entirely different type of boy. With David Copperfield, Dickens had explored the source of success. With Pip he explored the source of discontent. He portrayed Pip as guilty, fearful, anxious, and sensitive. Dickens drew a parallel between Pip's dream of becoming a gentleman using money he had not earned and the selfish expectations of Victorian society. Dickens put Pip and society on trial and found both lacking.

Great Expectations also draws upon Dickens's childhood experiences. This time he was more analytical in exploring his own youthful shame about his father's imprisonment and his work at Warren's. In many ways the story seems to be Dickens berating himself. For example, Pip tries to forget about his life as a black-smith; Dickens had tried to forget his work at the blacking factory. Dickens wanted to forget the poverty of his youth; Pip becomes a social snob and forgets the friends of his childhood. Pip's final acceptance of the black-smith Joe and the convict Magwitch as father figures he

Magwitch from Great Expectations, *as depicted by Kyd, one of Dickens's illustrators.*

loves without shame seemed to suggest that Dickens finally acknowledged his love for his own father, who, despite financial inadequacies, had encouraged his son to become a gentleman.

In addition to a mystery that propelled the action forward, *Great Expectations* contained some of Dickens's best comedy. In a letter to Forster, Dickens said, "You will not have to complain of want of humour as in *A Tale of Two Cities."*

As he wrote, Dickens once again identified closely with his youthful fictional creation and suffered pain in his side. As soon as he finished the book, his pain went away. At the end, Dickens did something he had never done before. He changed the ending based upon advice from his friend Edward Bulwer-Lytton. The new ending reflected a more hopeful future for Pip and Estella and may have indicated Dickens's desire for a warmer relationship with Nelly Ternan. Not until John Forster's biography of Dickens was released was the original ending of *Great Expectations* revealed—and many read-

From the original Household Edition, illustrated by F. A. Fraser, a scene from Great Expectations *in which Pip, Miss Havisham, and Estella talk by the fire.* (Dickens House Museum, London)

ers thought it better suited to the characters and the plot.

Dickens's readers identified with the Victorian belief that education, social status, and prosperity were worthwhile goals. By having Pip's goals revealed to be self-deceiving and provided by a criminal source, Dickens questioned these Victorian values. Despite its pessimistic tone, the book was an immediate success. Dickens had returned to the humor of his earlier years, and critics hailed the novel as having the best traits of both his early and later works. Sales of *All the Year Round* once again reached 100,000 copies per week.

The first installment of *Great Expectations* appeared in December of 1860, a few days after Abraham Lincoln was elected president of the United States, touching off the spark that would lead to the American Civil War. Dickens thought the war would be a short one. However, some believed that Great Britain might enter the war on the side of the South because British textile manufacturers needed a steady supply of cotton. If that happened, Dickens figured that when the war ended he would be too old to go to America again. When a friend asked him if he planned an American reading tour, Dickens responded: "Think of reading in America? Lord bless you, I think of reading in the deepest depth of the lowest crater in the Moon, on my way there!"

❧ DICKENS'S CHARACTERS ❧

Ebenezer Scrooge. Tiny Tim. Pip. David Copperfield. Oliver Twist. Uriah Heep. Charles Dickens created nearly one thousand characters. Many of them are still instantly recognizable today. One of the ways he imprinted his characters so deeply in our minds was his choice of memorable names: Serjeant Buzfuz, Hannibal Chollop, Luke Honeythunder, the Jellybys, Kit Nubbles, Dolge Orlick, Charity and Mercy Pecksniff, Pumblechook, Zephaniah Scadder, Peg Sliderskew, Mr. and Mrs. Spottletoe, Dick Swiveller, Prince Turveydrop. Dickens sometimes named characters after people he knew. He also found names in guest books, on headstones, or in the court papers he documented as a reporter.

Some names are puns: Pip's beloved is called Estella, which is a play on the word "star"; Miss Havisham, from the same novel, is herself a sham. "Mr. Grimwig" is a cranky character; "M'Choakumchild" is an evil headmaster. Most of all, Dickens wanted his characters' names to be descriptive and to make their role in the story easy to grasp.

In September 1863, Dickens's mother died after many years of illness. She had lived with her son Alfred's widow, who had agreed to care for her if Charles provided a house for them. Although Dickens visited his mother from time to time, the visits were difficult because her mind was confused: "My mother, who was also left to me when my father died . . . is in the strangest state of mind from senile decay."

There was no warmth in the relationship between Dickens and his mother, whom he had never forgiven for wanting him to continue working at Warren's Blacking Factory. He observed no mourning period after her death, and the inscription on her tomb might have been written for a stranger: HERE ALSO LIE THE REMAINS OF ELIZABETH DICKENS WHO DIED SEPTEMBER 12TH 1863 AGED 73 YEARS.

On Christmas Day, Dickens learned of another death: that of his longtime friend and rival, William Thackeray. The two had been estranged for five years until a few weeks before Thackeray's death. Dickens's daughter Kate was instrumental in encouraging them to reconcile. One night, both men were in a theater lobby at intermission. Thackeray walked up to Dickens and said: "It is time this foolish estrangement should cease . . . we should be to each other what we used to be. Come; shake hands." Dickens took Thackeray's proffered hand.

Dickens continued to have frosty relationships with his children. When he learned that his son Walter had died in Calcutta on New Year's Day from a ruptured aorta,

Walter Landor Dickens.

he sent an inscription for Walter's tomb but did not communicate any kind of sympathy to Catherine, who grieved deeply. Six months later, Dickens received a request from the colonel of Walter's regiment to pay his son's remaining debts. Most of Dickens's sons seemed to have inherited their grandfather's inability to manage money.

As he grew older, Dickens began to withdraw into himself. He still favored the brightly colored clothes of his youth and still surrounded himself with friends, but he was exceedingly private about his personal relationships. It is believed that he continued to be close to Nelly Ternan, and at some point she became his mistress, but the details of their affair were jealously guarded. His work had given him fame and fortune, and he had learned the downsides to both.

Six

Curtain Calls

———◆———

Dickens persuaded Nelly Ternan to give up her career as an actress and rented a house near his own for her, her mother, and her sisters. He introduced her to Georgina and his daughters. Sometimes he disappeared for days or weeks, visiting friends or taking Nelly on trips.

Although his desire to write another book was strong, his energy was not. The combination of Dickens's health problems, his disappointment in his sons, and the strain of keeping his relationship with Nelly out of the public eye made him feel much older than his fifty-two years. He had not written a novel long enough for monthly installments since *Little Dorrit,* ten years before. For the first time in over twenty-five years, "Phiz" was not his illustrator. Dickens had replaced Hablot Browne with a younger, more modern illustrator, Marcus Stone.

As he struggled to begin a new book, Dickens realized that he must now plan a story carefully instead of being able to rely on bursts of creativity. He also suffered a swollen foot that he blamed on frostbite, but it was actually a warning of more serious health problems to come.

Once he finally started on the book that became *Our Mutual Friend,* Dickens developed a complex plot in which dustheaps, or garbage mounds, and the polluted Thames River, both sources of wealth in nineteenth-century Britain, served as unifying symbols of the corrupting power of the desire for money. Dickens sharply attacked those poisoned by a greed and an ambition that caused them to reduce everything, including human life, to a monetary value.

When serialization began in May 1865, opening sales for *Our Mutual Friend* exceeded any of the earlier ones—but by the last installment twenty months later, sales had dropped drastically. E. S. Dallas, reviewing the novel in the *Times* six months after its serialization began, attributed the drop in readership to a weak beginning with too many characters that had no clear connection to the plot. Henry James, just beginning his own writing career, called *Our Mutual Friend* the "poorest of Mr. Dickens's works," claiming that it seemed forced and lacked inspiration. Whatever the reason for the drop in sales, publishers Chapman and Hall lost money on one of Dickens's books for the first time ever.

As with the reviews of Dickens's own day, modern criticisms also vary from "one of the greatest works of prose ever written" to "a failed genius." One critic saw *Our Mutual Friend* as a novel ahead of its time—setting the stage for future growth of great corporations, increased government control, and dwindling concern for people. After the attacks on greed and class prejudice, Dickens ended the novel on a hopeful note—the main characters have wealth and respectability, qualities Dickens himself pursued.

In June, while Dickens was still writing the last installments of *Our Mutual Friend,* he traveled to France by train with Nelly and her mother. As they returned home, a bridge collapsed and the train went off the rails between Dover and London. The carriage in which Dickens and his companions rode did not fall completely off the rail but hung suspended over one side of the bridge. Dickens was not hurt and managed to get out and then rescue Nelly and her mother. He returned to the car one more time to retrieve a manuscript, probably *Our Mutual Friend.* Then he spent hours helping the injured travelers. Fifty were hurt and ten died. Working among the injured and the dying took a heavy emotional toll. From that time on, Dickens hated traveling by train.

His daughter Mamie, who still lived with him at Gad's Hill Place, said, "My father's nerves never really were the same again . . . we have often seen him, when traveling home from London, suddenly fall into a paroxysm of fear, tremble all over, clutch the arms of the

A painting of Mamie Dickens done in 1868.

railway carriage, large beads of perspiration standing on his face, and suffer agonies of terror. We never spoke to him, but would touch his hand gently now and then. He had, however, apparently no idea of our presence; he saw nothing for a time but that most awful scene."

In February 1866, Dickens saw Dr. Frank Beard for a physical examination that revealed problems with his heart. The doctor prescribed medication and a less strenuous schedule. Dickens instead made plans for a series of thirty readings in and around London. They were more profitable than writing a new book. But by June, he was complaining of exhaustion and pains in his left eye, hand, and foot.

In October, Dickens learned of the death of his brother Augustus, or "Boz." Dickens had favored his youngest sibling by helping to pay for his education and getting him a secure job. However, Augustus never settled down and flitted from job to job, piling up debts. Finally, Augustus had deserted his family—a wife who had just gone blind and a son—to go to the United States. There he took advantage of Charles's fame by using the nickname "Boz" to schedule a series of Shakespearean lectures.

As Augustus traveled about the lecture circuit, the woman he had eloped with after deserting his wife accompanied him. In America he referred to this woman as his wife, and they eventually had three children. Unable to support himself, he asked Dickens for assistance. But Charles had already taken over the support of Augustus's family in London. Dickens cut off communication with his brother, thinking that contact kept Augustus hopeful for financial aid. Augustus died before the brothers could reconcile.

In 1867, despite exhaustion and the pain of his weakening health, Dickens decided to make a second trip to the United States. He was offered a minimum of 10,000 pounds for a reading tour and could not afford to turn it down.

At a farewell dinner, Dickens was overcome by emotion at the sight of more than five hundred people gathered to wish him well. He was immensely popular in England, beloved by readers across class divisions and by his peers. Through his tears, Dickens told them, "Your resounding cheers just now would have been but so many cruel reproaches to me if I could not here declare that, from the earliest days of my career down to this proud night, I have always tried to be true to my calling." Dickens's calling, it seems, was to offer the world in which he lived a fanciful, comic, but faithful mirror in which to see some version of itself.

The major obstacle to Dickens's American trip, besides his health, was that he did not want to be separated from Nelly. He worked hard to find a way for her to accompany him, but nothing would do. He decided to go without her and then see if there was some way she could follow. Before he sailed for America, they arranged for a coded telegram to be sent through Wills. If Dickens wrote "All well," Nelly should follow him to the United States. If he wrote "Safe and well," she should not. When Dickens arrived in America, he told his American publisher about Nelly. Three days later Dickens sent a telegram: "Safe and well."

This trip to the United States was a success. His readings drew large, enthusiastic crowds, including more than 40,000 people in New York alone. But when people who had seen him on his previous trip twenty-five years before met him again, they saw an aged man in pain. Shortly after arriving, his health began a precipitous decline—his left foot swelled so much that he could not get his shoe on. To save his energy, he accepted few

BUYING TICKETS FOR THE DICKENS READINGS AT STEINWAY HALL.

In this 1867 wood engraving, Americans mob the box office to purchase tickets for a Dickens reading in Boston. (Library of Congress)

social engagements and resorted to increasing doses of laudanum (opium dissolved in alcohol) to help him sleep. The many famous figures that wanted to meet him, including President Andrew Johnson, often had to be content with attending his readings.

In April, he gave his last American reading. The audience "stood cheering and tearful as, gravely bowing, and refusing all assistance, as if in that final moment he wished to confront us alone, the master lingered and lingered, and slowly retired."

Dickens had earned much more than the original

This photograph of Dickens was taken during his 1867 trip to America.

10,000 pounds promised. When he returned home, he was a rich but very sick man. His left foot, hand, and arm felt strange, and he had sudden dizzy spells. He did not realize that he was having little strokes. He was just grateful to be reunited with Nelly, whom he continued to keep a closely guarded secret.

Dickens rested at Gad's Hill Place during the month of May, but by June was ramping up his workload again. His assistant at *All the Year Round,* William Wills, had fallen from his horse in a hunting accident while Dickens was in America and suffered a concussion. He was unable to return to work. No one had done anything with the business side of the magazine in Dickens's absence. In some ways, however, Wills's accident proved to be fortunate. Dickens's oldest son Charley had gone bankrupt, having lost money on a paper mill business for which Angela Burdett-Coutts had provided the capital. Charley still owed one thousand pounds and had a wife and five children to support. At age thirty-one, he did not have a job or an income. He asked his father to let him work on the magazine. In November, Dickens made Charley a sub-editor, and the younger Dickens eventually took over many of Wills's duties.

That fall, Dickens's youngest son, Edward (Plorn), left for Australia. A shy, sensitive boy since childhood, the sixteen-year-old had little energy or real ability. Edward had already accepted that he could not measure up to his father's expectations, saying, "Sons of great men are not usually as great as their fathers. You cannot get two Charles Dickens in one generation."

When it came time for him to leave, Dickens wrote a farewell letter to Edward and gave him a check for two hundred pounds: "I need not tell you that I love you dearly, and am very sorry in my heart to part with you. But this life is half made up of partings, and these pains must be borne. . . . As your brothers have gone away, one by one, I have written to each such words as I am now writing to you . . . I hope you will always be able to say in after life, that you had a kind father."

The actual parting at the station was emotional for both Dickens and his son. Dickens was surprised at how much the departure affected him. As the train pulled away, Plorn "seemed . . . to become once more [the] . . . youngest and favourite child . . . and I did not think I could have been so shaken."

Plorn took a complete set of his father's works to Australia. Later, when Plorn's gambling got him into trouble in the outback and his debts mounted, Dickens was angry and felt betrayed. The two never saw each other again.

The week before Plorn's departure, Henry had enrolled at Cambridge. His father had agreed to pay his actual expenses but to provide no extras. Despite the fact that Henry was the only one of his sons who had any ambition or goals, Dickens told him, "We must have no shadow of debt. . . . You know how hard I work for what I get, and I think you know that I never had money help from any human creature after I was a child. You know that you are one of many heavy charges on me, and that I trust your so exercising your abilities and improving the advantages of your past expensive education, as soon to diminish *this* charge."

When Henry received an annual scholarship of fifty pounds to study law, he was elated, thinking he would not have to budget so carefully. Dickens proudly received this news from his son but then cut Henry's allowance by the amount of the scholarship.

In late summer, Dickens began preparation for what would be his last tour. He wanted a new reading selection and decided to prepare the scene from *Oliver Twist* in which the criminal Bill Sikes murders his companion, Nancy, after he discovers she has become an informer to the police. In a graphic, emotional scene, he grabs "her by the head and throat, dragged her into the middle of the room, and . . . placed his heavy hand upon her mouth." He strikes her upturned face twice with his pistol, then "[s]he staggered and fell, blinded with the blood that rained down from a deep cut in her forehead." Sikes uses a heavy club to deliver a fatal blow. In the morning, when sunlight shines on Nancy's body, Sikes turns his back, unable to face what he has done: "He . . . kindled a fire, and thrust the club into it to burn away and smoulder to ashes. He washed himself and rubbed his clothes; where the spots would not be removed he cut the pieces out and burnt them."

Dickens had previously considered the piece too violent to recite, but for his last tour he decided to risk everything. He began by practicing in the yard at Gad's Hill Place, where his piercing screams and groans scared those who heard him. One time, while he was working in the library, Charley heard the commotion and rushed outside, looking for the source of the horrible noises. He was brought up short to find it was just his father in rehearsal. Charley told his father it was "the finest thing I have ever heard, but don't do it."

On October 6, Dickens began the reading tour at St. James Hall but became hoarse and nauseated afterwards. He forced himself to continue but did not dare attempt the death of Nancy.

Dickens reading from his work in the late 1860s. (Dickens House Museum, London)

Dickens approached several of his friends about including Nancy's murder scene in the readings. Most of them were opposed. Finally, the Chappells, who had arranged his last London tour, suggested that Dickens give a private performance for a select audience to test their reaction. Dickens agreed and, on November 14 at St. James Hall, presented the reading to about one hundred guests. His performance horrified the audience, but ninety of the guests told him, "It must be done."

A few days later, a minister in attendance wrote to

Dickens that the reading was "a most amazing and terrific thing, but I am bound to tell you that I had an almost irresistible impulse upon me to *scream,* and that, if anyone had cried out, I am certain I should have followed."

Dickens's health worsened. He was still having problems with his left side, had trouble sleeping, and experienced frequent nausea. Adding the murder scene to his readings might have further damaged his health. It was a physical and emotional drain on his energy. Yet he refused to listen to reason and began to "murder" Nancy on an almost nightly basis

By February 1869, his left foot was totally lame. He had to cancel a reading and spent some time resting at Gad's Hill Place, where he made changes to his will. The new one included a legacy of one thousand pounds for Nelly Ternan and continued provisions for Catherine and for Mary, as long as she did not wed. Dickens left Georgina eight thousand pounds and most of his personal jewelry and private papers. He bequeathed his library and his interest in *All the Year Round* to Charley. To his longtime good friend John Forster, he willed his favorite watch and named him the official Dickens biographer.

Dickens resumed the reading tour but was having obvious physical and mental problems. During one reading he was unable to pronounce the name of his first famous character, Pickwick. He tried "'Picksnick,' 'Picnic,' 'Peckswicks,' . . . everything but 'Pickwick.'" As he

MR. CHARLES DICKENS'S
Farewell Readings.

Mr. CHARLES DICKENS has resumed his Series of Farewell Readings at

ST. JAMES'S HALL, PICCADILLY.

The Readings will take place as follows:

TUESDAY EVENING, FEBRUARY 8, The Story of Little Dombey (last time) and Mr. Bob Sawyer's Party (from Pickwick).

TUESDAY EVENING, FEBRUARY 15, Boots at the Holly Tree Inn; Sikes and Nancy (from Oliver Twist); and Mrs. Gamp (last time).

TUESDAY EVENING, FEBRUARY 22, Nicholas Nickleby (at Mr. Squeers's School, last time); and Mr. Chops, the Dwarf (last time).

TUESDAY EVENING, MARCH 1, David Copperfield (last time), and The Trial from Pickwick.

TUESDAY EVENING, MARCH 8, Boots at the Holly Tree Inn (last time); Sikes and Nancy (from Oliver Twist, last time); and Mr. Bob Sawyer's Party (from Pickwick, last time).

TUESDAY EVENING, MARCH 15, FINAL FAREWELL READING, The Christmas Carol (last time), and The Trial from Pickwick (last time).

To commence each Evening at Eight o'Clock.

No Readings will take place out of London.

PRICES OF ADMISSION:

SOFA STALLS, 7s.; STALLS, 5s.; BALCONY, 3s.;
Admission—ONE SHILLING.

Tickets may be obtained at CHAPPELL & Co.'s, 50, New Bond Street.

A poster promoting a few of Dickens's planned farewell readings. (Dickens House Museum, London)

stumbled repeatedly trying to capture the right word, he looked stunned. Later he blamed the medication he was taking.

After that, Charley took on the responsibility of watching his father during each performance. Dickens's doctor instructed him, "You must be there every night, and, if you see your father falter in the least, you must run and catch him and bring him off to me, or by Heaven, he'll die before them all."

The tour continued to take its toll. A friend who had not seen him in a while was astonished: "He looked desperately aged and worn; the lines in his cheeks and round the eyes, always noticeable, were now deep furrows, there was a weariness in his gaze and a general air of fatigue and depression about him."

Despite his worsening condition, on March 9 Dickens had a private visit with Queen Victoria at Buckingham Palace. She had been a fan of his since attending a private showing of *The Frozen Deep* in 1857 and had purchased a copy of *A Christmas Carol* for her private library. The interview lasted an hour and a half.

Dickens planned to give his last reading, number seventy-two out of the originally planned one hundred, on March 15. When news reached the public that Dickens would be giving his last performance that evening, huge crowds gathered outside St. James Hall. Over 2,000 people jammed into the building, leaving hundreds of others standing in the street.

At exactly eight o'clock, Dickens walked onto the stage, wearing formal evening dress and clutching tightly his book of readings. At his appearance, the audience rose in a standing ovation, cheering for several minutes. Charley later said, "I thought I had never heard him read . . . so well and with so little effort."

Dickens gave a second reading that brought the audience to its feet again in a prolonged period of cheering and applause that made the chandeliers shake. Dickens left the stage, but the adoring audience called him back again and again. When they finally quieted, Dickens delivered a brief speech: "Ladies and Gentlemen, it would be worse than idle—for it would be hypocritical and unfeeling—if I were to disguise that I close this episode in my life with feelings of very considerable pain." After reviewing his years of public readings and announcing the forthcoming publication of *The Mystery of Edwin Drood,* Dickens concluded: "From these garish lights I vanish now for ever more, with a heartfelt, grateful, respectful, and affectionate farewell."

Again the audience rose, cheering and applauding. With tears running down his cheeks, Dickens walked away. But the audience wanted one more glimpse. He returned to the stage and blew a kiss to them before leaving for the last time.

Seven

Farewell to a Great Spirit

---◆---

Back at Gad's Hill Place, Dickens was writing his fifteenth novel, *The Mystery of Edwin Drood*. This was his first book in four and a half years. In order to conserve his energy, he planned the story to be his shortest one, serialized in twelve parts instead of the usual nineteen. Despite his mental confusion during some of his last readings, Kate later claimed, "My father's brain was more than usually clear and bright during the writing of *Edwin Drood*."

Despite his failing health, Dickens continued to take an active interest in the lives of the people of England—particularly the underclasses. Now the most famous author in the country, if not the world, Dickens could no longer assume fake names to investigate social abuses. He was escorted into the seamier parts of London by a

This engraved print by Samuel Hollyer shows Dickens writing in his study at Gad's Hill Place. (Library of Congress)

police guard. There he discovered the opium dens that would open the pages of *Edwin Drood* and witnessed the extreme hunger and want of London's poorest residents.

The Reform Bill of 1867 had finally fulfilled some of the requests of the People's Charter, adding nearly one million new voters to the rolls. But the challenges of industrialization were not being met. Poverty was rampant, and it would be another year before the 1870 Education Act made free education available to most children. Dickens could not forget those who still languished in need and, in addition to dramatizing their plight, continued to support relief efforts.

Dickens worked carefully on the construction of *Edwin Drood* but found he was using up incidents too fast. The first two installments were each short by twelve pages. Still, the first episode of the serialization sold 50,000 copies.

Whether *Edwin Drood* would have been a masterful culmination of Dickens's themes showing "his imaginative power . . . at its best"; a venture into the new detective-story genre; or, as a friend and fellow novelist claimed, a "last laboured effort, the melancholy work of a worn-out brain," the manuscript is the only unfinished work in the great body of Charles Dickens's writings.

In early May, Dickens attended a formal banquet for the Prince of Wales. Attendants had to help Dickens into the dining room and carry him upstairs to the reception. By May 11, his foot bothered him so much he canceled his dinner engagements for the next week. On June 5, Kate arrived for a visit with her father and was alarmed at how he had changed. Although he was talkative and cheerful, he was exhausted after a short walk in the garden. Kate had come to ask his advice about taking up a career as an actress. Her husband was ill and they needed money.

Dickens begged her not to go on the stage and offered her a substantial sum of money. They talked into the early hours of the morning. Dickens told her that he hoped for great things from *The Mystery of Edwin Drood,* "if, please God, I live to finish it . . . I say if, because, you know, my dear child, I have not been strong lately."

He also told her that he wished that he had been "a better father, and a better man."

The next morning, Kate interrupted her father's writing to tell him good-bye. Usually when he was working, he simply held up a cheek for a quick kiss and did not talk. That morning he hugged her and said, "God bless, you, Katie!" She started out the door and got as far as the front porch. Something told her to go back. When Dickens saw that she had returned, he got up, hugged and kissed her.

On June 8, Dickens made plans to go to London the next day on business and then worked the rest of the day on *Edwin Drood*. That evening, when he came to dinner, his sister-in-law Georgina noticed that he looked different and inquired if he was ill. He replied that he had been very sick for the past hour or so. She asked him if he wanted to lie down. He replied, "Yes, on the ground," before he collapsed on the floor. Georgina got servants to help her lift him onto a couch. She called Mamie, Katie, Charley, Nelly Ternan, and the local doctor. All night Dickens lay on the sofa, breathing heavily.

The next morning Charley arrived with a specialist, but nothing could be done. Dickens had suffered a paralytic stroke and never regained consciousness. He died at 6:10 PM, exactly five years after the railroad accident. He was fifty-eight years old.

Prior to his death, Dickens had issued orders about his funeral: "I emphatically direct that I be buried in an inexpensive, unostentatious and strictly private man-

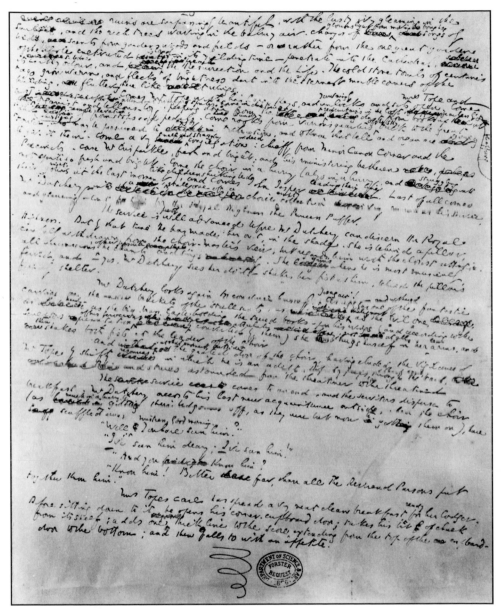

The last page of Dickens's unfinished manuscript, The Mystery of Edwin Drood. (Courtesy of the Victoria & Albert Museum, London / Art Resource.)

ner; that no public announcement be made of the time or place of my burial; that at the utmost not more than three plain mourning coaches be employed; and that those who attend my funeral wear no scarf, cloak, black bow, long hat band, or other such revolting absurdity."

The London *Times* begged to differ and recommended his burial in Westminster Abbey: "Westminster Abbey is the peculiar resting place of English literary genius, and among those whose sacred dust lies there . . . very few are more worthy than Charles Dickens of such an honor."

On June 14, a special train took his body from Gad's Hill Place to Charing Cross Station. From there a hearse transported the coffin to Westminster Abbey, where private funeral services were held in keeping with Dickens's wishes. His daughters Kate and Mamie, his sons Charley and Henry, and his sister-in-law Georgina attended. Catherine Dickens, his wife of thirty-three years and the mother of his ten children, was not among the mourners.

On the day of his funeral, shops were closed and bells tolled. His grave remained open for three days as thousands of people passed by, tossing flowers of all kinds on top of the coffin. The pit was soon filled to overflowing. Dickens was laid to final rest in Poet's Corner, Westminster Abbey.

From the United States came this message from Henry Wadsworth Longfellow: "Dickens was so full of life that it did not seem possible he could die . . . I never knew an author's death to cause such general mourning. It is no exaggeration to say that this whole country is stricken with grief."

Crowds gather in Poet's Corner at Westminster Abbey to view Dickens's grave.

Dickens's estate amounted to about 93,000 pounds, almost half of which he had earned from his public reading tours. John Forster and Georgina were his executors. The bulk of it, including the copyrights to his books, was divided evenly among his surviving children. Each received about 6,000 to 8,000 pounds.

Georgina Hogarth in her old age.

After Dickens died, his son Henry published two books and an article about his famous father. Charley continued Dickens's tradition of giving public readings and published several reminiscences of his own.

Georgina, Dickens's sister-in-law, and Mamie, his daughter, shared a home for many years. Together they edited the first collection of Dickens's letters (1880-82). Georgina spent her life guarding Dickens's memory, defending both his life and his works. She maintained contact with his children, reconciled with Catherine, and remained friends with Nelly. Georgina, who died in 1917, outlived all of the children for whom she had cared except Kate and Henry.

Kate lived to old age. In 1929, she gave interviews to Gladys Storey that became the basis for *Dickens and Daughter* (1939). It was the first book to reveal details of Dickens's relationship with Nelly Ternan and helped scholars learn a little more about the famous author's personal life.

In 1876, Nelly Ternan married a clergyman, twenty-eight-year-old George W. Robinson, who later became the headmaster of a school. During their courtship, she told Robinson that she was twenty-six, a decade younger than she really was. The couple had two children, Geoffrey and Gladys. Nelly died in 1914, forty-four years after Dickens's death. Not until over twenty years later did the public learn the extent of her relationship with Charles Dickens.

Catherine Dickens had not been invited to her husband's funeral. After Dickens's death, she was allowed to visit Gad's Hill Place, where she enjoyed several Christmases with Charley's family, including visiting with her eight grandchildren.

Kate took care of her mother until Catherine's death on November 21, 1879. Kate listened to her mother's complaints about Dickens and tried to help her remember the good times with him. Just before she died, Catherine gave Kate a bundle of letters from Dickens, written to her during their engagement and the early years of their marriage. She told Kate, "Give these to the

British Museum—that the world may know he loved me once." Although John Forster did not picture Catherine favorably in his authorized biography of his longtime friend, more recent biographers have seen her in a less critical light.

The nineteenth century was rife with outstanding authors, artists, and musicians. Charles Dickens rose above them all to be the most recognized English author after William Shakespeare. The curator at No. 48 Doughty Street, one of Dickens's residences in London and now the headquarters of the Dickens Fellowship, which keeps his memory alive and promotes his works, explained why she believed Dickens was so special: "It's his human touch. He knew so much about people. And although he was a gigantic literary figure, he retained the fresh view of a child."

Even though disillusioned time and again by those he loved and by his own expectations, Dickens remained in touch with the essence of humanity. He loved people. His obituary read: "He was of the people, and lived among them. . . . In the open air of the streets, and woods, and fields, he lived, and had his being, and so he came into closer union with common men, and caught with an intuitive force and fullness of feature every detail of their daily life. His creations . . . are familiar to every man, high or low."

The imaginary worlds Dickens created often seemed

Opposite: Dickens's Dream, *an 1870 painting by Robert William Buss, which depicts the author surrounded by visions of his characters.* (Dickens House Museum, London)

more alive to him than his actual life. As his oldest son Charley once said, "The children of his brain were much more real to him at times than we were." If history judges him as a man, he was probably no better or worse than most. However, if history judges him by the imaginary worlds and the unforgettable characters that he created, then he was indeed "The Inimitable Boz."

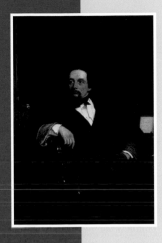

TIMELINE

1845	Alfred D'Orsay Tennyson Dickens is born; *The Cricket on the Hearth* is published.
1846	First monthly part of *Dombey and Son* is published.
1847	Sydney Smith Haldemand Dickens is born; Dickens's sister Fanny dies.
1848	Henry Fielding Dickens is born.
1849	First installment of *David Copperfield* serial is published.
1850	Dora Annie Dickens is born; *Household Words* is published.
1851	John Dickens dies; daughter Dora Annie Dickens dies; Dickens produces play, *Not so Bad as We Seem.*
1852	Edward Bulwer Lytton Dickens is born; first installment of *Bleak House* appears.
1853	Dickens gives first public reading of *A Christmas Carol.*
1854	First installment of *Hard Times* is published.
1855	Dickens meets with Maria Beadnell; first installment of *Little Dorrit* is published.
1856	Dickens purchases Gad's Hill Place.
1857	Dickens family and friends give benefit performance of *The Frozen Deep;* Dickens meets Ellen "Nelly" Ternan.
1858	Separates from wife Catherine; starts extensive reading tour in England.
1859	Starts new weekly journal, *All the Year Round;* begins serialization of *A Tale of Two Cities.*
1860	Brother Alfred dies; Dickens moves permanently to Gad's Hill Place; burns twenty years' accumulation of letters and papers; first installment of *Great Expectations* is published.
1863	Dickens's mother, Elizabeth Barrow Dickens, dies; son Walter dies in India.
1864	Publishes first installment of *Our Mutual Friend.*
1865	Dickens escapes unhurt from train wreck.
1866	Brother Augustus (Boz) dies.

1867 Dickens makes second trip to America.

1868 Son Edward (Plorn) leaves for Australia; Dickens's last surviving brother, Fred, dies.

1869 Dickens starts last novel, *The Mystery of Edwin Drood;* gives last public reading. Dickens dies on June 9.

SOURCES

CHAPTER ONE: Early Years

p. 10, "That I suffered . . ." Michael Allen, *Charles Dickens' Childhood* (London: Macmillan Press Ltd., 1988), 87.

p. 16, "What would I . . ." Angus Wilson, *The World of Charles Dickens* (New York: Viking Press, 1970), 49.

p. 18, "My father and . . ." Norrie Epstein, *The Friendly Dickens* (New York: Viking Penguin, 1998), 22.

p. 20, "no advice . . ." Ibid., 25.

p. 21, "I never afterwards . . ." Edgar Johnson, *Charles Dickens: His Tragedy and Triumph,* vol. 1 (New York: Simon & Schuster, 1952), 44.

p. 21-22, "I got a little . . ." Charles Dickens, *David Copperfield* (Hertfordshire, UK: Wordsworth Editions Limited, 1992), 201.

p. 23, "viciously drawing . . ." Johnson, *Charles Dickens,* 49.

CHAPTER TWO: Back to Work

p. 25, "exceedingly good . . ." Fred Kaplan, *Dickens: A Biography* (Baltimore: Johns Hopkins Press, 1988), 47.

p. 30, "Ah, Mr. Dickens . . ." Catherine Peters, *Charles Dickens* (Gloucestershire, UK: Sutton Publishing Limited, 1998), 16.

p. 32, "My existence . . ." Wilson, *The World of Charles Dickens,* 101.

p. 32, "I never have . . ." David Paroissien, *Selected Letters of Charles Dickens* (Boston: Twayne Publishers, 1985), 32.

p. 37, "I should like . . ." Norman MacKenzie and Jeanne MacKenzie, *Dickens: A Life* (New York: Oxford University Press, 1979), 42.

p. 43, "needy admirers flattened . . ." Peter Ackroyd, *Dickens* (New York: HarperCollins Publishers, 1990), 196.

p. 47-49, "[Oliver] rose . . ." Charles Dickens, *Oliver Twist* (Ashland, OH: Landoll, 1993), 14.

p. 49, "I wished to show . . ." George Gissing, *Critical Studies of the Works of Charles Dickens* (New York: Greenberg, Publishers, Inc., 1924), 50-51.

p. 49, "I don't *like* . . ." MacKenzie, *Dickens: A Life,* 57.

CHAPTER THREE: Making a Name

p. 52-53, "The dear girl . . ." Paroissien, *Selected Letters,* 37.

p. 56, "It will be our aim . . ." Gissing, *Critical Studies,* 59.

p. 59, "And so it always . . ." MacKenzie, *Dickens: A Life,* 79.

p. 60, "I do swear . . ." Ibid., 80.

p. 63, "Old wounds . . ." Paul Schlicke, ed., *Oxford Reader's Companion to Dickens* (New York: Oxford University Press, 1999), 434.

p. 63, "Nobody will miss . . ." MacKenzie, *Dickens: A Life,* 98.

p. 67, "It is a great trial . . ." Wilson, *The World of Charles Dickens,* 114.

p. 68, "It would be a triumph . . ." Johnson, *Charles Dickens,* 352.

p. 69, "How can I give . . ." Ackroyd, *Dickens,* 346.

p. 71, "I really don't think . . ." John Forster, *The Life of Charles Dickens,* vol. 1 (Philadelphia: J. B. Lippincott Company, 1890), 353.

p. 73, "I think *Chuzzlewit* . . ." Lyn Pykett, *Critical Issues: Charles Dickens* (New York: Palgrave, 2002), 79.

p. 74, "The thought of . . ." MacKenzie, *Dickens: A Life,* 137.

p. 74, "If you would reward . . ." Schlicke, *Oxford Reader's Companion,* 214.

p. 75, "held in three most . . ." Johnson, *Charles Dickens,* 461.

p. 76, "a squeezing, wrenching . . ." Charles Dickens, *A Christmas Carol* (Mahwah, NJ: Watermill Press, 1980), 3.

p. 76, "an angel . . ." Ibid., 116.

CHAPTER FOUR: Changing Times

p. 84, "If any of my books . . ." Schlicke, *Oxford Reader's Companion,* 185.

p. 86, "all but at the top . . ." Paul Davis, *Charles Dickens A to Z* (New York: Checkmark Books, 1998), 384.

p. 88, "If I were to say . . ." Schlicke, *Oxford Reader's Companion,* 151.

p. 88, "the best of all . . ." MacKenzie, *Dickens: A Life,* 225.

p. 92, "in the dirtiest . . ." Kaplan, *Dickens,* 270.

p. 92, "might be made . . ." Ibid.

p. 93, "My wife has presented . . ." Epstein, *The Friendly Dickens,* 355.

p. 95, "habit of suppression . . ." Peters, *Charles Dickens,* 67.

CHAPTER FIVE: Turning Points

p. 100-101, "Poor Catherine . . ." Paroissien, *Selected Letters,* 123.

p. 101, "a great fat lady . . ." Schlicke, *Oxford Reader's Companion,* 160.

p. 102, "Your father has asked . . ." Epstein, *The Friendly Dickens,* 301.

p. 103, "Nothing on earth . . ." Kaplan, *Dickens,* 388.

p. 103, "Don't suppose . . ." Ackroyd, *Dickens,* 812.

p. 103, "We were all . . ." Epstein, *The Friendly Dickens,* 302.

p. 109, "a dish of puppy . . ." Schlicke, *Oxford Reader's Companion,* 564.

p. 111, "But for me . . ." Ackroyd, *Dickens,* 876.

p. 111, "I rest my claims . . ." MacKenzie, *Dickens: A Life,* 391.

p. 111, "Would to God . . ." Johnson, *Charles Dickens,* 2:963.

p. 114, "You will not have . . ." Schlicke, *Oxford Reader's Companion,* 263.

p. 116, "Think of reading . . ." Kaplan, *Dickens,* 483.

p. 117, "My mother who . . ." Kaplan, *Dickens,* 424.

p. 117, "It is time . . ." Ibid., 453.

CHAPTER SIX: Curtain Calls

p. 120, "poorest of . . ." Henry James, "Our Mutual Friend," *The Nation,* December 21, 1865, http://humwww.ucsc.edu/dickens/OMF/dandOMF.html (accessed April 18, 2005).

p. 121, "one of the greatest . . . failed genius," Schlicke, *Oxford Reader's Companion,* 446.

p. 121-122, "My father's nerves . . ." Ackroyd, *Dickens,* 963.

p. 124, "Your resounding cheers . . ." Ibid., 1007.

p. 125, "stood cheering and tearful . . ." Ibid., 1022.

p. 127, "Sons of great . . ." Ibid., 878.

p. 127, "I need not tell . . ." Paroissien, *Selected Letters,* 167-168.

p. 128, "seemed . . . to become . . ." Edgar Johnson, *Charles Dickens: His Tragedy and Triumph,* vol. 2 (New York: Simon & Schuster, 1952), 1101.

p. 128, "We must have no . . ." Paroissen, *Selected Letters,* 169-170.

p. 129, "her by the head . . ." Dickens, *Oliver Twist,* 156.

p. 129, "He . . . kindled a fire . . ." Ibid., 157.

p. 129, "the finest thing . . ." Johnson, *Charles Dickens,* vol. 2, 1102.

p. 130, "It must be done . . ." Kaplan, *Dickens,* 532.

p. 131, "a most amazing . . ." Johnson, *Charles Dickens,* vol. 2, 1103.

p. 131, "'Picksnick,' 'Picnic' . . ." Epstein, *The Friendly Dickens,* 371.

p. 133, "You must be . . ." Peter Ackroyd, *Dickens: Public Life and Private Passion* (New York: Hydra Publishing, 2003), 208.

p. 133, "He looked desperately . . ." MacKenzie, *Dickens: A Life,* 377.

p. 133, "I thought I had . . ." Ackroyd, *Dickens,* 1066.

p. 134, "Ladies and Gentlemen . . ." Ibid., 1067.

p. 134, "From these garish . . ." Kaplan, *Dickens,* 549.

CHAPTER SEVEN: Farewell to a Great Spirit

p. 135, "My father's brain . . ." Ackroyd, *Dickens,* 1064.

p. 137, "his imaginative power . . ." Schlicke, *Oxford Reader's Companion,* 402.

p. 137, "last laboured . . ." MacKenzie, *Dickens: A Life,* 384.

p. 137, "if, please God . . ." Wilson, *The World of Charles Dickens,* 296.

p. 138, "a better father . . ." Epstein, *The Friendly Dickens,* 372.

p. 138, "God bless . . ." Kaplan, *Dickens,* 553.

p. 138, "Yes, on the . . ." Epstein, *The Friendly Dickens,* 373.

p. 138-140, "I emphatically direct . . ." Kaplan, *Dickens,* 543.

p. 140, "Westminster Abbey . . ." Johnson, *Charles Dickens,* vol. 2, 1156.

p. 140, "Dickens was so full . . ." Ibid., 1154-1155.

p. 143-144, "Give these to . . ." Schlicke, *Oxford Reader's Companion,* 162.

p. 144, "It's his human . . ." Richard W. Long, "The England of Charles Dickens." *National Geographic* (April 1974): 476.

p. 144, "He was of the people . . ." Martin Fido, *Charles Dickens: An Authentic Account of His Life & Times* (New York: The Hamlyn Publishing Group Ltd., 1970), 128.

p. 146, "The children of his . . ." Ackroyd, *Dickens,* 401.

BIBLIOGRAPHY

Ackroyd, Peter. *Dickens*. New York: HarperCollins Publishers, 1990.

————. *Dickens: Public Life and Private Passion*. New York: Hydra Publishing, 2003.

————. *Introduction to Dickens*. New York: Ballantine Books, 1991.

Allen, Michael. *Charles Dickens' Childhood*. London: Macmillan Press Ltd., 1988.

Chesterton, G. K. *Appreciations and Criticisms of the Works of Charles Dickens*. New York: Haskell House Publishers, Ltd., 1970.

Davis, Paul. *Charles Dickens A to Z*. New York: Checkmark Books, 1998.

Dickens, Charles. *A Christmas Carol*. Mahwah, NJ: Watermill Press, 1980.

————. *David Copperfield*. Hertfordshire, UK: Wordsworth Editions Limited, 1992.

————. *Oliver Twist*. Ashland, OH: Landoll, 1993.

Epstein, Norrie. *The Friendly Dickens*. New York: Viking Penguin, 1998.

Fido, Martin. *Charles Dickens: An Authentic Account of His Life and Times*. New York: The Hamlyn Publishing Group Ltd., 1970.

Forster, John. *The Life of Charles Dickens*. Vols. 1 and 2. Philadelphia: J. B. Lippincott Company, 1890.

Gissing, George. *Critical Studies of the Works of Charles Dickens*. New York: Greenberg, Publishers, Inc., 1924.

Hobsbaum, Philip. *A Reader's Guide to Charles Dickens*. New York: Farrar, Straus and Giroux, 1972.

James, Henry. "Our Mutual Friend." *The Nation,* December 21, 1865. http://humwww.ucsc.edu/dickens/OMF/dandOMF.html.

Johnson, Edgar. *Charles Dickens: His Tragedy and Triumph*. Vols. 1 and 2. New York: Simon & Schuster, 1952.

Kaplan, Fred. *Dickens: A Biography*. Baltimore: Johns Hopkins University Press, 1988.

Long, Richard W. "The England of Charles Dickens." *National Geographic* (April 1974): 443-483.

MacKenzie, Norman and Jeanne MacKenzie. *Dickens: A Life*. New York: Oxford University Press, 1979.

Paroissien, David, ed. *Selected Letters of Charles Dickens*. Boston: Twayne Publishing, 1985.

Peters, Catherine. *Charles Dickens*. Great Britain: Sutton Publishing Limited, 1998.

Pykett, Lyn. *Critical Issues: Charles Dickens*. New York: Palgrave, 2002.

Schlicke, Paul, ed. *Oxford Reader's Companion to Dickens*. New York: Oxford University Press, Inc., 1999.

Wilson, Angus. *The World of Charles Dickens*. New York: Viking Press, 1970.

WEB SITES

http://humwww.ucsc.edu/dickens/
The Dickens Project Web site, a University of California scholarly consortium devoted to promoting the study and enjoyment of his life, times, and works.

http://www.dickensmuseum.com
Offcial site of the Charles Dickens Museum in London.

http://www.victorianweb.org/authors/dickens/dickensov.html
An overview of the life and works of Charles Dickens.

INDEX